Children mature at differen … reading at different rates, but no child attending a State S… erate or semi-literate. Should this occur, the child has not failed, the school … d. Other school subjects have suffered as a result, and the child has met with a major setback in his life. With respect to the learning of reading the term "less able" is often an excuse for inadequate teaching.

This book contains a programme which enables parents to teach their children to read. It is intended mainly for parents of Infant-school children who are not reading, or have made very little progress in reading, by the age of 6½ to 7 years and where the school is not solving the problem. Modified versions of the same basic principles are suitable for teaching older children (Chapter 3) and adults to read, and for normal classroom teaching in Primary schools.

This teaching system has been proven over a long and specialised teaching career; it is derived from the writer's experience in Primary and Secondary schools as a class teacher, remedial teacher, Infant-school headmistress, remedial adviser, and lecturer to qualified teachers.

After retirement, and responding to requests for help from parents, the writer continued teaching children to read, on a one-to-one basis. More requests for such help led to the idea of showing parents how to teach their own children to read, with a weekly joint "review" lesson. These parents mentioned other children in need of similar help, confirming the writer's personal experience, and periodic reports in the media, that there is a fairly widespread, continuing need among schoolchildren for additional help in learning to read. This book was written so that more parents could teach their children successfully, thus providing help to many more children.

This book also includes sections on spelling and writing, which are introduced to the child at the appropriate time in his reading development. There are also chapters on teaching older children and dyslexic children to read. On glancing through the book don't be "put off" by the word-lists. These are very necessary and are accompanied by easy-to-follow rules.

The programme is designed to be enjoyable for the child, but to complete it successfully requires **dedication on the part of the parent** over a period of not less than 12 months and probably for as long as 18 months. It is recommended, but not essential to the success of this programme, that a parent works with her own child; however the choice of adult must meet family circumstances. If another adult carries out the programme with the child it is strongly recommended that a parent carries out, or sits in on, at least one session per week.

The programme consists of two main parts – "Look, Say and Remember" and Phonics, or word-building. The Phonics course is self-contained, but the "Look, Say and Remember" course requires reading books, either borrowed from the school or local library, or purchased (see Appendix 5).

This book is dedicated to my son Raymond, who has given me constant advice and encouragement during its preparation. Grateful thanks are due to Ginn & Co. for their permission to incorporate some of the phonic principles contained in earlier editions of their 'Beacon Readers' series. Many thanks are also due to Ute Mallon, Cyril Wilson and Mary Burgess for the preparation and review of the typescript.

For the sake of convenience only, the term 'he' is used throughout the book for the child and 'she' for the parent.

Contents

Chapter 1

Introduction

Reading is a skill which has to be taught. Today the term "teaching reading" is rarely used in schools. It has been replaced by the term "hearing reading", an entirely different function which is inadequate for acquiring the skill of reading. A summary of current methods, their origins and limitations, is included in Appendix 3.

This teaching programme is based on traditional lines, which no longer exist in most Primary Schools; modified versions of the 'Look and Say' and phonic methods are used. The latter technique is introduced only when a child is ready to learn by this method; using it too early will meet with failure.

Each stage in the system is carefully developed so that at no time will the parent be at a disadvantage with the instructions. The programme has been used to teach many hundreds of children of all ages to become fluent readers.

Why Involve Parents?

Increasingly, disclosures of the inadequate standard of reading in our schools are being reported in the media. Gone are the days when a school was proud of its high reading achievements, its standards in spelling, grammar, writing, tables and maths. These basic subjects always had priority. Primary schools emphasising their importance can be found, but they are regrettably in the minority. It is a sad reflection on modern teaching that the most important subject in a child's early school life, namely learning to read, is so neglected. It is pushed aside to make time for other, child-centered, activities.

Countless parents are truly dissatisfied with the current teaching at Primary Level and extremely worried about their children's future. The cry of "Back to Basics" is becoming louder, but how long will it take for this to be heard? How many more children will leave Secondary schools with no qualifications and a limited future?

While the education experts ponder the merits of one method or another, this does not give immediate help to the children who are not responding to prevailing systems. If a child has reached the age of 6½ to 7 years, and is still not making noticeable progress, and if the school is not solving the problem, it is perhaps time for the parents to take the matter into their own hands. If a child is not reading by the age of seven he begins to fall behind in some other school subjects, sometimes irreversibly.

As an example, in March of 1990 a mother came to see me asking for help. Her little boy was 6 years 2 months old. She had just been told by his teacher that he was a "plodder" and would never be a "high flyer". When asked what he did during "silent reading", which is practised in his Primary School, the teacher replied "he just looked at the ceiling". His non-verbal I.Q. was high, but the only word he could recognise was "a". His mother followed all the instructions in this book. She sat in at the weekly lessons with the writer, which were a revision of the work she had done with her boy during the week. During holidays she gave only a short daily lesson. By the end of September 1990 he had read in and out of context over 1000 words. He had learnt these words by "Look, Say and Remember" plus phonic work. In his books he had read 560 sentences, most of which were not just simple sentences. Since that time he has progressed steadily to become a fluent reader. His is not an isolated case.

Perhaps many parents have tried to help their child, but became discouraged because they, too, were making no progress. This will not happen if this book is followed carefully. As progress is made and the simplicity of the techniques discovered, both parent and child will experience great enjoyment and a sense of achievement.

Dyslexia

In recent years the word "dyslexia" has become widely known. Many children, not yet reading under the 'Look and Say' method as practised in many schools, are often falsely labelled "dyslexic". This is a tremendous worry for parents, who do not know how to cope with the situation.

There are two considerations to be borne in mind. Firstly, **real dyslexia** is a comparatively rare condition; secondly, with proper tuition it can be corrected.

The following experiences of the author over a six year period in the Remedial Department of a Secondary school illustrates the rarity of this condition. Together with one colleague, 480 eleven-year-old children, either non-readers or semi-literate, were taught to read during their first year in that school, using the teaching methods in this book. At the end of each year, with the exception of four or five of them, the children left the Remedial Department with high "reading ages". The few requiring further help stayed on until they too had high reading ages. In all that time, with all those children, a "dyslexic" child was never found.

But dyslexia does exist and the truly dyslexic child needs specialised tuition to overcome it. Chapter 4 describes the method developed by Doctor Grace Fernald who has made an outstanding contribution to teaching dyslexic children how to read.

Be aware that dyslexia is not fully understood, and test methods are imprecise. Also, some conditions often confused with dyslexia can be remedied in a simple manner, described under 'Non-Dyslexic Difficulties' in Chapter 4. Before considering the procedures of Dr Fernald, first try the standard system in this book, carefully and patiently; it has worked for many children who were incorrectly diagnosed as dyslexic.

Chapter 2
The Teaching Programme

Introduction

Children mature mentally at different rates, and attempting to teach a child to read before he is mentally ready will end in failure. Readiness to read is also dependent on the development of some physical attributes, and certain social and emotional features. There are three distinct stages in the teaching of reading, and as a child matures mentally he will move through them. Thus, the teaching programme comprises three parts, corresponding to these stages:-

Part 1. Pre-reading Activities/Getting Ready for Reading.

Part 2. "Look, Say and Remember" plus Single Sounds.

Part 3. Word-building/Phonic Approach.

Pre-reading activities in schools are designed to pave the way for the learning of reading, and most children are ready for Part 2 between the ages of $5^1/_2$ and 6.

The main thrusts of this programme are Parts 2 and 3. The third Part is introduced after a defined amount of progress has been made with Part 2, **and from that point both Parts continue in parallel until the programme is completed. The two techniques are complementary, not competitive, but success in phonic work demands more mental maturity than the "Look, Say and Remember" technique, and will not be successful if introduced too early.**

The key feature of the "Look, Say and Remember" part of this programme is the emphasis on checking that the words have been properly learnt, i.e. the 'Remember' element of the technique. This checking routine is turned into a game as far as the child is concerned, **but it is the most important element of this teaching method.** The original technique, used in many schools from the 1960's, is called 'Look and Say'; few schools now give this emphasis on checking the learnt words, without which the rate of retention by the child is low.

The third part, phonics or word-building, is the most important part of this programme. As the teaching of phonic work progresses it is a delight to see the child reading out many of the new words for himself, using the simple little rules developed for this system. No longer is it necessary for him to be told all the new words. The more phonic rules he absorbs the more fluent his reading becomes. At the end of this part the child has become more familiar with all the rules and has finished the mechanical process of learning to read. **The introduction of the phonic approach speeds up the learning process dramatically, and is also a tremendous asset as an aid to good spelling.**

How to get the best out of this Programme

A final word of advice. It is **extremely important** that a child learning to read must read **every day.** He must have continuous contact with the printed word, **even if it is only a few sentences per day.** Once this programme is begun it must be continued **daily.** This involves self-discipline on the part of the parent. However, your enthusiasm and the child's immediate success and enjoyment of the programme will provide the stimulus to continue.

The following six points are important for success:-

1. To avoid conflicts with other activities, choose a set time of day suitable to both you and the child. **Always start at the set time.** Some parents prefer early morning, before school, when the child is more alert, but it depends on the running of the household.
2. Make sure the child is neither tired nor hungry.
3. The length of each Daily Session depends on the concentration of the child, which will vary from day to day. **STOP** when the child is losing concentration. You will soon judge how much he can do in a session.
4. The child will enjoy the Daily Sessions if you go at his pace.
5. **Never let the child experience failure.** Make light of it if he forgets a word. There is always another chance.
6. **Praise must be given continually to establish and maintain confidence.**

The Teaching Programme Part 1 — Pre-reading Activities or Getting Ready for Reading

In this book we are mainly concerned with Parts 2 and 3 of the teaching programme. However, we will have a brief look at Part 1 here.

In this stage the child experiences various activities which lay a good foundation for the teaching of reading. It begins in the home and is continued in much greater depth at the beginning of a child's life at school. The three most important factors to be considered in the home are speech, vocabulary and vision which, if developed in the home, will be an excellent preparation for school life.

Speech

"Baby Talk" and forms of careless speech must be replaced by articulate speech. Correct the child if he mis-pronounces a word; such a word must be said to the child slowly and distinctly until he says it correctly. Perseverance with this will bring success.

Vocabulary

To enlarge the child's vocabulary, he must be spoken to at every available opportunity, introducing him to new words daily. His vocabulary can be greatly increased by looking at books with pictures, discussing them and repeating the names of the contents of the picture. This is also stimulating the child's interest in books.

Vision

Obviously eye-sight is of paramount importance if the child is to experience success in reading. Sight is tested within the first few months of attendance at school, and any problems are resolved at that time.

The development of vision, so that a child can look at the different shapes of letters and recognise them, progresses as the child matures. This is greatly helped by training the child in eye habits which help him to look at words from left to right. Long before the child begins to read he can be taught to look at print from left to right. If an adult is reading to him the book can be shared so that the child can look at the adult pointing to each word in a left-to-right direction. Short simple stories that the child enjoys hold his interest and extend his concentration.

Play schools and nursery schools help a great deal in these respects. Pre-reading training in infant schools is usually carried out well, ensuring that speech, vocabulary and eye-habits are well established by the age of six. Any physical disabilities relating to eye-sight, hearing etc. are normally identified and resolved at this stage.

The Teaching Programme Part 2 — "Look, Say and Remember", plus Single Sounds Course

This "Look, Say and Remember" course is preferably carried out with the two reading schemes mentioned in Appendix 5, which are carefully graded for word difficulty and repetition. If other well-graded reading **schemes** are being used in the school, they may be used instead; consult the teacher. Note that some teachers prefer that their school material is not used in ways other than specified by themselves, but many welcome external help. The only materials required are strips of paper (12" x 4"), twenty cardboard squares measuring 2" x 2", a black-felt-tip pen, and a folder.

Except for older children who are following the programme sequence described in Chapter 3, this course must be started with the **first book of the first reading scheme,** designed for a six year-old child, regardless of the age and reading ability of the child when starting the course.

For general planning of the teaching sessions please study carefully the section **'How to get the best out of this Programme'** earlier in this chapter.

The sequence of events for learning the words, and checking the learned words, of the first three sentences in the first reading book, is shown below in five lessons. This is followed by three lessons (6–8) showing the teaching procedure for the next three sentences.

The First Lesson of the "Look, Say and Remember" course will take two or three 'Daily Sessions' to complete, as will the Second Lesson. Each of lessons 3, 4 and 5 may take one 'Daily Session'. **The important thing is to move forward at the pace of the child throughout all of the "Look, Say and Remember" Course. Progress depends on many factors, including the age and skills of the child, and pressing on too quickly will not result in success.**

The First Reading Book

"Look, Say and Remember" — The First Lesson

Now that you are ready to start, sit down with the child and discuss the first reading book, looking at the first illustration, telling him you are going to help him to read his new book and that soon he will be able to read it by himself.

Read the first sentence, which is usually very short, pointing to each word as it is spoken. Read it several times, getting the child to point to each word. Now, get the child to say the sentence, pointing to every word. At this stage, of course, he is only memorising the words in "parrot" fashion. Now he will "read" the first sentence, remembering every word. Repeat this procedure until three sentences have been "read" in this manner, which may take two or three 'Daily Sessions'. For example the sentences could be:-

Here is a shell.
Here is another shell.
Here is the sea.

"Look, Say and Remember" — The Second Lesson

The aim of the Second Lesson, which is a partial repetition of the First Lesson, is to make sure the child can read the sentences of the First Lesson by himself.

Using a book-mark, which might be just a folded piece of paper, cover up all the sentences on the first page, except the first one. The child must now point to each word, saying it by himself. He will proceed in like manner with the other two sentences, pointing to each word. This is continued until you are sure the child knows all the words in the three sentences. This may take two or three 'Daily Sessions.'

"Look, Say and Remember" — The Third Lesson

Before starting this lesson, print each word from the Second Lesson on strips of paper (12" x 4"), in large letters, one word per strip, as shown below. Mark the page number from the book **in a corner** of each strip for easy reference.

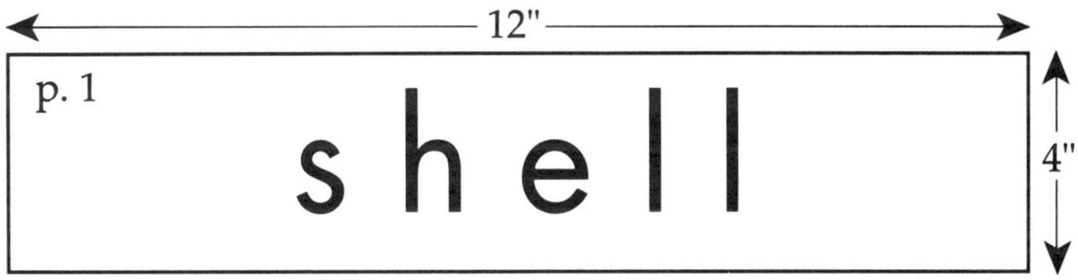

The **letter style** to be used for the paper strips is shown here:-

a b c d e f g h

i j k l m n o p

q r s t u v w x

y z

The child repeats the Second Lesson, reading the first three sentences in the book, and then closes the book. Place the strips of paper mentioned above face up, either on a table or on the floor, in the same formation as the first three sentences in the book. The child will read them without difficulty. Even if he does forget a word, open the book immediately, **without showing any disapproval,** find the word and get the child to read the sentence again. **At no time from now on must the child experience failure.**

"Look, Say and Remember" — The Fourth Lesson

The child repeats the Second Lesson, reading the first three sentences in the book, and then closes the book. Now mix up the strips of paper and spread them out face down. Ask the child to pick up any one and say the word that is printed on it. As you proceed, place correctly recognised "words" in one pile, which the child has "won", and incorrectly recognised "words" in another pile.

Remembering the words has become a game and the child really enjoys it. If he knows the word, he keeps it. If he has forgotten any word there should be no sign of displeasure by the parent.

The next stage of the revision 'game' is to re-attempt the incorrectly recognized "words". Turn the strips with these unknown words face up and spread them out. Open the book and find each word from the page number marked on the strip of paper. To jog his memory, let the child read the sentence containing the forgotten word , with him pointing to and repeating the unknown word several times. Do this until all the forgotten words have been read again. Now ask the child for any word in the "forgotten" pile which is still spread out, face up. When he has "won" these, turn them over, mixing them up. Ask him to pick up any one, turn it over and read it. Repeat if necessary, until he has "won" the "forgotten" pile.

"Look, Say and Remember" — The Fifth Lesson

The child reads the first three sentences in the book, and closes the book. To make doubly sure that the child knows these words, put all the strips together in a bundle, face down, in any order; show them to the child one at a time and ask him to say the word on the strip. Again, as you proceed, place correctly recognised "words" in one pile and incorrectly recognised "words" in another pile.

As previously, on completion find any "unknown" words in the book and get the child to read the appropriate sentence again, with him pointing to and repeating the unknown word several times. Then ask the child for any word in the "forgotten" pile, showing the paper strips to him one at a time. When he has "won" all the words the revision 'game' is finished.

When this lesson is successfully completed, you are sure that the words from the first three sentences are properly known.

"Look, Say and Remember" — The Sixth Lesson

After the first three sentences in the first reading book have been completed, it is no longer necessary to read all new work to the child as was done in the First Lesson. This is because, in a properly graded reading scheme, new work uses many of the words already fully learned by the child. It is also unnecessary to lay out the paper strips in sentence formation as was carried out in the Third Lesson. For the rest of the first reading book only three lessons (6–8) are used for new work.

In this, the Sixth Lesson, the child re-reads the first three sentences in the reading book. He then attempts the new work (the second three sentences). He will recognise some of the words from the previous work. When he hesitates over a new word, tell it to him to maintain the fluency of the reading. The child then re-reads the sentences in which there were "unknown" words.

Keep a note of each **new** word to be learned. If the book is your own, lightly pencil a circle round each word. Print each **new** word on strips of paper (12" x 4"), in large letters, one word per strip, as shown previously. Mark the page number from the book **in a corner** of each strip for easy reference.

"Look, Say and Remember" — The Seventh and Eighth Lessons

The new work is followed by the two checking procedures described earlier in lessons four and five, which train the child to remember words and increase his reading vocabulary. **Only the new words from the new work are checked with these procedures.**

Completing the First Book

The first book is completed in the manner described in Lessons 6 to 8, except that before starting any new work, the child **always** re-reads **all** the sentences from **all** previous lessons.

When the first reading book is completed, **check the child on all the words in the book,** using the procedure described in Lesson 5. If he is successful he has "won" his new book. If any word has to be learned again, use the procedure described in Lesson 5.

It is essential to make sure that the child knows every word in the books because, if not taught by the procedures described above, children can go through the early books just by memorising each page. Time and time again it has been taken for granted that a child is reading very well when it is found out that he cannot recognise each individual word. Some children can "read" with the book unopened; one child "read" an entire book at home when the book was at school!

The Second Reading Book and Subsequent Reading Books

The First Lesson

Prior to the start of the new book a little talk about it paves the way and will sustain interest. In a good reading scheme there will be repetition of words already known. This means that the child will begin to read the first two or three words. When he comes to a "new" word, you supply it. This keeps the fluency of the reading going. Draw a circle round the "new" word while telling it to the child. **Proceed in this manner until seven new words have been told. This completes the First Lesson.**

As previously, transfer these "new" words to large strips of paper and mark the page number in the corner of the strip, ready for the next lesson.

The Second Lesson

This lesson is spent learning the "new" words that were printed on paper strips during the First Lesson. In these early stages these words have to be repeated several times, pointing to and reading the word on each strip. When the repetition of the new words is satisfactory, put the strips down, face up, in random order. Say one of the words and ask the child to point to it. If he is correct he has "won" the word and lifts up the strip. Do this with the remaining words, praising him for all the words that he has remembered.

Should some of the words remain unrecognised open the book and ask him to read the sentence or sentences containing the word or words that he has forgotten. A little extra repetition must be done on those words. Now place the seven strips face down in random order and ask the child to pick up any one he likes and say the word written on it. He does this until he has said the seven new words.

Lastly, put the strips in random order in a bundle. Sit facing the child and hold up one strip at a time so that the child sees the word. If he gets the word right, he keeps the paper strip. Continue until he has "won" the seven words.

The Third Lesson

Open the book again. The child will now read from the beginning until he has covered the seven "new" words. Continue with the reading until the next seven "new" words have been ringed. Use the same checking procedures as described in Lesson 2. After each set of "new" words has been checked in this manner and "won" by the child, he re-reads the sentences containing them before proceeding to the new work.

The Last Lesson of each Book

When the book is finished place all the strips in a bundle face down. The child is now trying to "win" all his "words". Sit facing him and hold the strips up one by one. If there are one or two "forgotten" words he is reassured that he will have another chance. The "forgotten" words are usually few in number. Put them to one side, ready for the second chance. Praise him for winning such a large bundle of words. Find the "forgotten" words on the appropriate pages in the book. A short revision time on these words is generally sufficient. To vary the 'game' put the "forgotten" words behind your back and ask the child which arm he would like. The child usually succeeds now at the first attempt; he has "won" all his "words" and is ready for the next book.

Throughout the rest of the "Look, Say and Remember" course these four lessons are the pattern for all reading books.

Single Sounds

The child may know the sounds of all the letters, but we are assuming here that they need to be taught.

Single sounds are usually introduced after the third book of the recommended series "One, Two, Three and Away!", and are normally completed after the sixth, seventh or eighth book.

At this stage make no reference to the **name** of the letter, only its **sound.** The single letter sounds used in this method are illustrated in the following list. Vowels are sounded in their 'short' form; most consonants are sounded as if there was a short 'u' appended to them. Note that the letter 'q' is presented as 'qu', as it is always used in this way.

a	as in	sat	n	as in	nut
b	as in	but	o	as in	off
c	as in	cut	p	as in	pup
d	as in	duck	qu	as in	quack
e	as in	egg	r	as in	run
f	as in	fun	s	as in	sun
g	as in	gun	t	as in	tub
h	as in	hug	u	as in	uncle
i	as in	is	v	as in	vulcan
j	as in	jug	w	as in	won
k	as in	kung fu	x	as in	xerox
l	as in	lug	y	as in	young
m	as in	mud	z	as in	zebra

The letters have been grouped in a specific sequence below, ready for the time when word-building (phonics) will begin. Note that the vowels are placed in "boxes", explained below. The sounds qu, v, x, y and z are learned later, at Stage 4 of the Phonics Course. **The order of presentation of the sounds must not be changed.**

Set 1 s f h t p n m r [a]

Set 2 b [i]

Set 3 c l [o]

Set 4 g [u]

Set 5 k w [e] d j

Method

1. At the top of a sheet of unlined paper, using a black-felt-tip pen, print a large letter "s" (approx. 1" x 1"). Let the child trace the letter with his index finger (using the hand with which he writes), sounding it as he traces it.

   Now, using a pencil, lightly print on the same page, twenty to thirty times, a smaller size of "s", approx. $\frac{3}{4}$" tall. Alternatively, fill the page with a series of dots in the form of the letter "s". Then let the child trace over each "s" with a black-felt-tip pen, sounding "s" as he traces it.

   This is, simultaneously, the beginning of the process of learning to write. Cursive ('joined-up') writing begins later, during the phonic stage of learning to read.

2. Print an "s" on a cardboard square (2" x 2") using a black-felt-tip pen. Ask the child to say the sound.

3. If he sounds it correctly he can keep the cardboard square — he has "won" the sound. Place it in an envelope or a small container; on the outside write "Set 1, s".

Continue in this fashion until the child has learnt the next three sounds, ("f", then "h", then "t") and has "won" them. Before another sound is learnt, take out the cardboard squares with the "already known" sounds on them, and ask the child to sound them again, to make sure he has remembered them. Familiar words in the child's vocabulary will help him remember the sound, e.g. sun, sock, soap etc. will help with the sound "s". After successful revision of these first four sounds, proceed with the next four sounds in Set 1, using the three-stage method described above. Revise these last four sounds before moving on to "a", the final sound in Set 1.

Now print a large letter "a" at the top of a sheet of paper, and place a box around it. Explain to the child that the "a" is in a box because it is special, and is called Special "a". Then follow the three-step method described above. When the child has learnt Special "a", he is ready to revise all the sounds in the first Set, using the procedure described below.

Lay out on the table the cardboard squares with the letters from the first set, in the same 'left-to-right' sequence shown above. Ask the child to sound each letter, moving from left to right, which was the order in which they were taught. When this is successful, mix up the cardboard squares and place them face down, asking the child to pick up any one and sound the letter written on it. Continue this until the child has "won" the whole Set. Because the child has sounded and written the letters many times, he should "win" the Set easily. However, should a sound be forgotton, repeat both procedures described in this paragraph.

When you are sure he knows Set 1 continue with the remainder of the sets, always making sure to do revision, as described above, until all the sets are known. This is a gradual process and should be carried out in parallel with "Look, Say and Remember" work. Be sure he knows the vowels are Special — a, e, i, o, u.

Moving on to Phonic Work

When a child has finished learning the single sounds, his "Look, Say and Remember" work is well established. The child now proceeds to the last technique which is Phonic Development.

It is incorrect to say that the child learns either by "Look, Say and Remember" or by phonics. He learns by a combination of both methods. While the child is learning his word-building he still continues with the "Look, Say and Remember" technique.

From the time that phonic work starts, each Daily Lesson must include time devoted to both courses.

It is interesting to note that after the child has mastered the single sounds, when he is reading he often tries to get an unknown word by sounding its first letter. **This is usually an indication that he is ready to move on to phonic work.**

However, the phonic programme requires a certain mental maturity for success in mastering the rules, and children mature mentally at their own pace. Trying to do phonic work before a child is mentally ready will only meet with disappointment and loss of the confidence which has been growing since experiencing success with "Look, Say and Remember". The first stage of the phonic programme includes advice on judging whether or not the child is ready for phonics. **Do not neglect this advice.**

The Teaching Programme Part 3 — Phonics (Word-Building) Course

Since 96% of the English language is phonic it is clear that the mastery of phonic rules will hasten completion of the process of learning to read. The following phonic tables are so well graded that the child will not experience failure once he has grasped the idea that if he sounds his letters he can make words.

Ninety-three phonic tables or sets are grouped into nine initial stages. Little rules introduce some of the stages, to help the child work through the tables easily. An additional eighteen phonic tables follow these nine stages, to complete the phonic programme.

STAGE 1

There are 20 Sets in Stage 1. The method for teaching the first Set is described below in detail. Discontinue the use of cardboard squares (Steps 1–3 of the method) after Set 5 of Stage 1. The letters and words used in Set 1 are as follows:-

Stage 1, Set 1 **s f h t p n m r [a]**

sat	tap	nap	ran
sap	tan	ma(ss)	ram
Sam	Tam	mat	as
fat	Pat	map	at
fan	pat	man	an
hat	Pam	rat	am
ham	pan	rap	

Method

1. For the nine single letters in Set 1 above, lay out the cardboard squares (2" x 2") that were used earlier in the learning of single sounds. Lay them out in a row, in the sequence shown above.

   Get the child to sound each letter, which is thoroughly known from the earlier learning of the single sounds.

2. Placing the appropriate cardboard squares from the row together, form the word "sat" with them.

   Get the child to sound the three letters several times, and then ask him what the little word says. He will probably say the word, "sat". Try this several times if he is unsuccessful at first.

   If he still cannot say the word, move the cardboard letter "t" approximately 2" to the right. Sound the letters "s" and "a" together, pronouncing them to the child as one sound, "sa", followed by the "t", i.e. "sa-t". Try several times, but if he is unsuccessful **do not continue.**

   This introduction to phonic work usually presents no problem after single sounds have been mastered. However, if the child is hesitant over sounding this word by either of the above techniques, do not press him any further. **He has in no way failed. He is just not ready, as yet, to start with phonics.** Make light of this saying, "we'll do this another day".

   Do not try to continue; it is important not to have failure at this point. Carry on with his "Look, Say and Remember" work, where he is experiencing success, and at the same time keep revising the single sounds. Try again in a few weeks' time and you will see the difference.

3. When the child is ready, continue in this fashion with the rest of the words in Set 1, **one word at a time,** e.g. sap, Sam, fat, etc. Explain the big "S" in "Sam" because it is the beginning of someone's name. The child is delighted with his success and will want to try to make more words.

   Note that if it was necessary to move the cardboard letter "t" to the right and blend the first two letters in order that the child succeeded with the first word, then the remainder of the set should be done in the same fashion. However, if the first approach was successful then it should be continued for the rest of the set.

   The meaning of each word, if not known, should be explained. The double (ss) should be explained (one sound).

4. Now print the nine letters of Set 1 at the top of a sheet of paper, with the "Special" vowel "a" enclosed in a box, as shown overleaf.

   Underneath the single letters print each word in Set 1, in **large letters** as presented overleaf, and ask the child to sound each little word and say it. Use either style (a) or (b) overleaf, depending on which of them was successful for the first word in the set (see Step 2 above).

5. Next, using the appropriate "style" overleaf, for each word the child says the three sounds "in his head" and then says the word aloud. Repeat this once or twice.

6. Then give the child an exercise book to copy down Set 1, using style (a) and the size of the letters overleaf, sounding each word silently and then reading it aloud after he has written it.

7. Proceed to Set 2 when these six steps are completed successfully.

Additional Instructions

1. For each Set in all Stages of the Phonic Programme start with the word at the top of the left-most column **and proceed vertically downwards;** then do the same with the next column, and so on.

2. The size of lettering used overleaf is used throughout the nine phonic stages. From Set 2 onwards style (a) overleaf is always used for the writing of words.

3. **Always explain the meaning of words that are not already known by the child.**

4. Writing the Set in an exercise book (step 6 above) is only employed for the first five Sets of Stage 1 unless, at your discretion, a Set requires attention.

5. For the rest of Stage 1, and for the other eight stages, each Set would usually be one lesson, but in some cases, where a Set comprises only a few words, a lesson could comprise two Sets.

Set 1

s f h t p n m r [a]

Style (a)

sat	tap	nap	ran
sap	tan	ma(ss)	ram
Sam	Tam	mat	as
fat	Pat	map	at
fan	pat	man	an
hat	Pam	rat	am
ham	pan	rap	

Style (b)

sa-t	ta-p	na-p	ra-n
sa-p	ta-n	ma-(ss)	ra-m
Sa-m	Ta-m	ma-t	a-s
fa-t	Pa-t	ma-p	a-t
fa-n	pa-t	ma-n	a-n
ha-t	Pa-m	ra-t	a-m
ha-m	pa-n	ra-p	

Stage 1 Sets 2–5

In Set 2, the letters "b" and "i" are introduced. With little children it can be said that "a" has worked so hard he has gone to sleep. Now all of Set 1 consonants plus "b" and "i" go to make the next set of words. This is the pattern throughout Stage 1. Set 3 introduces "c", "l", and "o". Set 4 introduces "g", "u" and Set 5 introduces the letters "k", "w", "e", "d" and "j". When the child has completed Set 5 he has made 141 words.

Stage 1, Set 2 **b [i]**

sit	hit	nip	bib
sip	Tim	mi(ss)	is
sin	tip	mi(tt)	it
fit	tin	rim	in
fin	pip	rip	if
his	pit	rib	
him	pin	bit	
hip	nib	bin	

Stage 1, Set 3 **c l [o]**

sob	pop	Bob
for	pot	cot
hot	not	lot
hop	mo(ss)	cob
hob	lo(ss)	o(ff)
top	mop	on
Tom	rot	
tot	Ron	

Stage 1, Set 4 **g [u]**

sun	hub	rug	gun
sum	tub	rut	gu(ll)
sup	tug	cup	us
fun	lu(ll)	cut	up
hut	nut	bus	
hum	nun	bun	
hu(ll)	mug	bug	
hug	run	gut	

Stage 1, Set 5 **k w [e] d j**

set	te(ll)	Ne(ll)	bet	led	we(ll)
se(ll)	Ted	Ned	bed	le(ss)	wet
fe(ll)	pen	men	be(ll)	let	wed
hen	peg	met	beg	get	den
hem	pet	jet	Ben	Ken	de(ll)
ten	net	red	leg	keg	fed

These five sets are followed by revision sets, below. It is left to your discretion whether the child should read up to Set 14 or not, depending on the fluency achieved by the child at this point.

The reason for so many sets of three letter words and the amount of repetition they contain is quite simply explained. **Three letter words are difficult to read,** because there is very little variation in the visual pattern, for example "bad, bed, bid, but". In longer words the wider variation of the pattern helps in decoding the word.

After Set 5 of Stage 1 introduce the child gradually to the **names** of the letters (excluding "qu, v, x, y, z"— these are introduced at Stage 4) in the order in which the sounds were learned. By the time he is ready for Stage 2 he will be familiar with the names of the letters.

At this point discontinue the use of cardboard squares.

Stage 1 Revision. Sets 6–14

Stage 1, Set 6

can	mat	cat	sat
sat	can	dad	sad
man	hat	mad	had
Dan	fat	sat	cat
fat	cap	hat	cap
hat	mad	had	fad
mat	map	Dan	hat
can	cat	hat	sat
Dan	dad	sad	fad
man	mat	had	fan
hat	mad	sat	fat

Stage 1, Set 7

tit	pin	win	pit
wit	tin	pin	wit
win	pit	wit	pip
tip	tip	tin	tin

Stage 1, Set 8

can	mad	had	fad
win	wit	hat	fan
tip	man	sad	fat
pit	pin	pip	tin
win	sad	fat	pip
wit	pip	tin	pit
had	pin	hat	can
fat	mad	win	Dan

Stage 1, Set 9

lop	ti(ll)	tip	win
do(ll)	Tim	lo(ll)	dot
pi(ll)	dot	wi(ll)	lot
not	don	tip	nod
ham	fan	sad	Sam
cat	pi(ll)	do(ll)	Tim
ti(ll)	Dan	wi(ll)	Dan
do(ll)	not	fat	Wi(ll)
lot	wig	ma(ss)	can
dog	pig	can	log
don	fag	hag	lo(ll)
lo(ss)	Sam	Tim	Tom

Stage 1, Set 10

bog	rut	fag	rug
jug	dog	Sam	jug
rug	ma(ss)	rut	mi(ss)
bo(ss)	man	run	wig
rum	pig	cap	jug
bog	pi(ll)	win	rum
lo(ss)	mat	rug	rut
bo(ss)	can	jut	run
yes	leg	box	fan
yet	rub	bag	gu(ll)
ye(ll)	gun	log	fad
keg	Lob	wig	jug

Stage 1, Set 11

fat	leg	do(ll)	fog
ti(ll)	rug	lo(ss)	Sam
led	nod	ti(ll)	Tim
yet	Len	le(ss)	lot
get	dot	pig	had
rum	tip	bog	Dan
Bob	box	gum	man
let	wig	has	cap
fig	had	tip	wig
pit	ham	tap	wag
pad	wit	ti(ll)	big
rid	fin	lit	ram

Stage 1, Set 12

cot	jog	him	not
hod	tap	do(ll)	pop
jam	bog	fan	pot
not	hid	hot	rip

Stage 1, Set 13

but	bud	top	fan
hu(ll)	pan	hut	wi(ll)
nut	pin	hit	hot
du(ll)	tin	fin	bin

Stage 1, Set 14

ten	man	sum	Sam
got	bad	rip	Tom
get	bed	mat	Wi(ll)
led	bid	hip	Gus
lad	bud	wed	Fan
fe(ll)	pen	dig	Ben
fi(ll)	pin	rub	Jim
fog	map	rum	Ken
met	sap	gum	Lob
mi(ss)	net	top	Mab
ti(ll)	dug	set	Ne(ll)
te(ll)	rob	sit	Dan
bi(ll)	set	sat	Pat

Stage 1, Set 15

Draw a box at the top of a sheet of paper and put an "s" inside it. Write down on the sheet some of the three-letter words that the child is familiar with, as follows:-

s

bat	fin	pot	rub
cap	hat	tip	bed
cat	dog	tin	peg
bin	doll	hut	rat
bat	mop	nut	gun
hill	let	sum	pot
pad	tap	tub	pen
tug	dig	mat	bun

The child says all these words.

Now tell the child that "s" is coming out of his box to visit his friends.

Write a small "s" behind the first word, to make the word "bats". The child now says, "bat-bats".

Repeat this procedure with the rest of the words in the set, cap-caps, cat-cats, bin-bins and so on, until the child has completed the set.

The child then reads the whole set to you.

It is interesting to note that at this stage the child is very capable of dealing with three-letter words and is able to cope with an extra consonant added on to them.

Stage 1, Set 15 s

bats	fins	pots	rubs
caps	hats	tips	beds
cats	dogs	tins	pegs
bins	dolls	huts	rats
bats	mops	nuts	guns
hills	lets	sums	pots
pads	taps	tubs	pens
tugs	digs	mats	buns

Stage 1 Sets 16–20 are all treated in the same way. The child sounds the first part of the word containing one vowel and adds the extra consonant at the end. This comes very easily to him.

The first three letters are written down in set form. They are sounded by the child and then the new letter "comes out of his box" and goes on to the end of the three-letter sounds e.g. "ben-bent" and so on.

Note that many of the initial sounds are not words as such, but are simply combinations of three letters; this presents no problem to the child.

Stage 1, Set 16 t

bent	must	lost	hunt
felt	dust	gift	rest
fist	rust	just	cost
melt	lent	left	punt
kilt	pat	nest	gilt
tent	mist	best	tent
dent	mint	lint	

Stage 1, Set 17 p

camp	rump	hump
damp	lump	rasp
lamp	help	sump
ramp	jump	pump

Stage 1, Set 18 d

band	sand	
land	tend	bend
hand	pond	wind
mend	fond	end
send	held	
lend	fund	

Stage 1, Set 19 m n

elm	film
helm	kiln

Stage 1, Set 20 **k**

milk	silk	rusk
tusk	dusk	bulk
task		

Stage 1 Revision. Sets 1–20

tins	sends	hunt	lift
mist	digs	pans	sift
film	must	camp	silk
lend	lend	lift	hump
melt	felt	ramp	runs
jump	helm	elm	tips
bins	went	milk	gasp
land	rest	sump	guns
held	help	lump	task
dust	tint	rusk	left
rubs	mend	lost	nest
sums	past	bulk	rugs
mats	mint	dusk	help
pond	dent	rump	pegs
hunt	west	last	dust

When the child has completed Set 20 he has to pass the above Revision Test before he can proceed to Stage 2. When he passes, the sheets containing all Stage 1 words are given to him to keep in a folder.

At the end of every successfully completed stage the child gets the sheets of words to put into his folder. These words are used later when learning spelling.

STAGE 2

Stage 2 covers double consonants at the end of a word (Sets 1, 3 and 4) and at the beginning of a word (Sets 7–16). In Sets 2, 5 and 6 the words have double consonants at the beginning or the end.

Stage 2, Sets 1 and 2

In Stage 2, Set 1 put a box at the top of a sheet of paper with two letters "ck" in the box.

Ask the child to sound "c" which he does. Ask him to sound "k" which he does. Explain that because both the letters sound "k" it is only necessary to say one "k".

Then write down sounds that the child is familiar with from the first stage, i.e. ba, ja, la, pa and so on.

"ck" then comes out of the box as usual, to visit his friends, "ba" becomes 'back', "Ja" becomes 'Jack' and so on until the set has been learnt.

The child then reads the set to you.

Set 2 is taught in the same manner, except that you sound the new double consonant sound "sh" for the child, repeating it until it is properly known by the child.

Stage 2, Set 1 **ck**

back	peck	sick	dock
Jack	neck	tick	sock
lack	deck	tock	duck
pack	Dick	lock	luck
tack	kick	cock	ruck
sack	lick	mock	wick
hack	pick	rock	suck

Stage 2, Set 2 **sh**

cash	sash	gush	shock
dash	ash	rush	shack
gash	dish	ship	shall
hash	fish	shin	shut
lash	wish	shop	shell
mash	mesh	shot	shed
rash	hush	shod	

Stage 2, Sets 3 and 4

Sets 3 and 4 can be learnt in the manner of Sets 1 and 2, but the new sounds "ng" and "nk" are two which the child might find a little difficult to pronounce.

To overcome this problem Set 3 can be introduced as "ang, ing, ong, ung", which the child learns easily. Write these three-letter sounds in boxes across the page, as follows:-

ang **ing** **ong** **ung**

They are learned separately, and when they are properly known the child reads the words in Set 3 without difficulty. He then has only to start each word with the single consonant sound, e.g. "sang, sing, song, sung".

Stage 2, Set 3

bang	ding	dong	hung
fang	king	long	lung
hang	ping	song	banging
gang	ring	tong	longing
pang	sing	rung	hanging
rang	ting	hung	singing
sang	wing	sung	ting-a-ling

Set 4 can be done in a similar manner. The three-letter sounds are of course:-

ank **ink** **unk**

Stage 2, Set 4

bank	link	wink	sunk	sink
rank	mink	bunk	rink	hunk
sank	pink	junk	tank	

Stage 2, Sets 5 and 6

For Set 5, place "ch" in a box at the top of a piece of paper, write the words of Set 5 underneath, and then teach this leading sound to the child. Then cover up the "ch" of the first word, with a finger. The child sounds the other part of the word, which he has met previously; as he does so, uncover the "ch" and the child sounds it, blending the two sounds together to sound the word. Repeat until the child is confident with the word. The same procedure is used for Set 6.

Stage 2, Set 5 **ch**

batch	fetch	rich	chip	chick
hatch	ketch	much	chop	check
catch	itch	such	chest	children
latch	ditch		chin	chug
match	hitch		chill	chink
patch	pitch		chap	chess
vetch	witch			

Stage 2, Set 6 **th**

bath	thin
path	thick
pith	thank
with	think
moth	thing

Stage 2, Sets 7–16

From Set 7, **and for the rest of the phonic programme,** it is no longer necessary to cover up parts of the word. Simply teach the new 'leading' sound and ask the child to read the Set.

Stage 2, Set 7 **wh**

when	whiff	whilst
whip	whisk	whir
which	whiskers	whirl

Stage 2, Set 8 **bl**

black	blush	block
bluff	blurt	blank
blunt	blur	blot

Stage 2, Set 9 **pr**

pram	prank	prim	prop
prick	press	prod	print

Stage 2, Set 10 **pl**

plank	plant	plot	plum	pluck
plan	plod	plug	plus	plop

Stage 2, Set 11 **tr**

tramp	trek	trick	truck
trap	trench	trip	trump
trash	trend	trot	track

Stage 2, Set 12 **br**

brag	bred	brim	brisk
brass	brick	bring	brush
brash	brill	brink	broth

Stage 2, Set 13 **cr**

crab	crack	crash	crib	cross	crush
crutch	craft	crept	crisp	crock	crust
crush	crank	crest	croft	crunch	crick

Stage 2, Set 14 **dr**

drag	drank	dress	drop	drum
drab	drink	drill	dross	drunk
draft	drench	drip	drug	drift

Stage 2, Set 15 **sp**

span	spar	speck	spick	spur
spot	spark	spend	spill	spurt
spank	spat	spell	spin	spurn

Stage 2, Set 16 **gl**

glad	gland	glum
glass	gloss	glint
glen	glut	glib

Stage 2 Revision. Sets 1–16

If the child reads Sets 5–16 without difficulty or hesitation, proceed to the revision words below. However, if the child is not reading these sets fluently it is advisable to carry out revision and reinforcement of the double consonant sounds.

If this is required, prepare paper squares, (2" x 2"), and write out all the initial sounds from Set 5 to Set 16, e.g. ch, th, wh, bl, etc. in **large print,** one sound per square. Make a game of learning these sounds in a similar way to the random testing used in the "Look, Say and Remember" approach. Spread the squares out face down; the child lifts them up one at a time and gives the correct sound.

Finally, Stage 2 revision is a very good test. The child reads perhaps fifteen to twenty words at a time. If he stumbles over any word he must go back to the particular set that introduced this rule and learn it again. When he passes Stage 2 he will get the sheets of words which make up Stage 2 to put in his folder.

cash	sank	sang	pack
dish	sink	sing	peck
shot	bank	sung	back
wish	bang	rang	deck
long	bank	song	sink
hush	pink	ring	neck
fish	rank	rung	duck
rush	sunk	king	pick
dash	wink	bang	rock
rock	bang	tick	pack
gush	tank	wing	sick
gash	link	hang	Jack
rich	catch	hitch	Dick
much	fetch	pitch	lock
black	crutch	brush	speck
prick	nest	crash	fleck
shock	drink	broth	bring
shack	stitch	cloth	fling
plank	flash	pluck	crack
trunk	shed	stick	thing
sang	whisk	sting	swing
cloth	stuck	bring	clock
broth	crutch	brick	truck
pluck	smack	crash	blank
children	thank	think	latch
church	thick	catch	check
punt	west	chum	shall
this	then	that	hitch
thing	shall	such	lock
think	rich	self	fetch
chick	lift	fond	just
which	past	hilt	glen
whist	rest	mend	hint

STAGE 3

Stage 3 is essentially a continuation of Stage 2. Here the child is faced with new double consonant sounds at the beginning of the words. It becomes quite easy now to sound and say the new word, e.g. "an" becomes span, "ill" becomes spill and so on.

All eleven sets comprise words in which two consonants go before a short vowel sound. To form each word, the child sounds the double consonant, adds the short vowel sound, and then completes each word, e.g. "st" → "sta" → "stamp". The three-letter combinations for the first word of each Set are shown in the heading for the Set.

Stage 3, Set 1 **st** → **sta**

stamp	stand	step	stick
stump	stung	stock	stilt
still	sting	stop	stack
staff	stem	stock	stitch

Stage 3, Set 2 **sp** → **spa**

span	speck	spend	spun
spat	spell	spent	spot
spank	spelt	spick	spurt
spill	spit	spin	

Stage 3, Set 3 **sn** → **sna**

snap	snatch	snip	snuff
snag	snick	snob	snug
snack	sniff	snub	snarl

Stage 3, Set 4 **sm** → **sma**

smack	smelt	smug	smash
smell	smock	smut	smirk

Stage 3, Set 5 **sl** → **sla**

slant	slat	slept	slop
slap	slag	slip	slot
slam	slash	sling	slug
slang	slump	slit	slim
slab	slush	slung	slept
slack	sled	slog	slick

Stage 3, Set 6 **sk** → **ski**

skim	skip	skimp	skunk
skill	skiff	sketch	skulk
skin	skid	skull	skimp

Stage 3, Set 7 **sw** → **swe**

swell	swam	swim	swish
swept	swig	swing	swot
swank	swill	switch	swirling

Stage 3, Set 8 **fl** → **fla**

flash	flung	fled	flush	flat	flick
flask	flint	fleck	fluff	fling	flit
flag	flinch	flop	flung	flesh	flock

Stage 3, Set 9 **fr** → **fra**

Frank	fret	frog
franc	frill	from
French	frisk	frost
fresh	frock	froth

Stage 3, Set 10 **tr** → **tra**

tram	trap	trim	truck
tramp	trash	trip	trunk
track	trend	trill	trust
tract	trench	trot	trump

Stage 3, Set 11 **pr** → **pri**

prim	prank	print
pram	press	prod
prig	prick	prop

STAGE 4

Here, for the first time, the child is introduced to three consonants before the vowel (the first three sets); he is also introduced to the last five **sounds,** i.e. "v, y, x, z, qu" (in Sets 4–8). After Sets 4–8 are completed, the child is introduced to the **names** of these five letters.

The same procedure is used as in the previous stages. The child is, at this stage, sounding and saying very well. As previously, the meanings of all new words included in the sets must be explained, e.g. "vandal", etc. The revision set for Stage 4 will ensure that the child has increased not only his phonic knowledge, but also his vocabulary.

Stage 4, Set 1 **spr**

sprat	spring	sprung
sprang	sprig	sprint

Stage 4, Set 2 **str**

string	strap	strong
strut	strict	stretch
strung	struck	strip

Stage 4, Set 3 **shr**

shrank	shrimp	shred
shrink	shrug	shrill

Stage 4, Set 4 **v**

van	vest	vandal	victim
vat	vent	vanilla	villa
vet	velvet	valiant	vulcan
vim	vagabond	vellum	

Stage 4, Set 5 **y**

yap	yank	yet
yes	yam	yelp
yell	yen	yak

Stage 4, Set 6 **x**

six	ox	lax	exact
fix	mix	fox	annex
flax	box	vex	boxer
tax	wax	text	

Stage 4, Set 7 **z**

zinc	zig	zip
zest	zeppelin	zag

Stage 4, Set 8 **qu**

quick	quiz	squint	quack
quest	quill	quench	quilt

Stage 4 Revision. Sets 1–8

visit	strap	shrimp	strut
yes	quack	yank	vagabond
shrank	sprat	velvet	quick
quill	shrink	shrug	strong
zinc	zag	victim	shred
yam	text	sprang	valiant
strung	sprig	exact	wax
sprat	fox	zest	quest
yet	squint	struck	string
spring	strict	vast	text
stretch	quilt	zig	sprung
vulcan	vex	strip	flax
shred	valid	villa	mix

STAGE 5

Before proceeding with Stage 5 it is now the time to teach three new words, **"Alphabet", "Consonants" and "Vowels".**

Write down these words. Ask the child to say the word "Alphabet"; he should do this several times, pointing to the word. When he can say it fluently introduce him to the word "Consonants". His early phonic training helps him to break up the word easily into three parts, "Con-son-ants". He says this word several times until he knows it. Lastly comes the word "Vowels". He points to the word and says it several times until he knows it.

Explain to the child that all the letters he has been learning, (their sounds and their names), are grouped together and are called the Alphabet. Write the word "Alphabet" again as a heading. Underneath write down all the letters, in small letters, in alphabetical order. The child finds no difficulty in saying these letters. Ask him to count the number of letters. He does so and finds that there are 26 letters altogether.

Draw a circle round each vowel sound, and **ask the child to say its name and its sound.** The child counts that there are five letters with a circle round them. These five letters have a special name. They are called Vowels and without them words cannot be made. They can be called the **Vowel Family.** The child says the names of the five vowels several times. Now the child finds out that there are 21 letters left. These have also a special name. They can be called the **Consonant Family.** The child repeats the **names** of these 21 letters several times.

Print the words 'Vowel Family' as a heading and underneath print the vowels. Then print the words 'Consonant Family' as a heading and underneath print the consonants. The child counts the number of letters in the **Vowel Family** and then you write the number 5 at the side with a circle round it. Lastly the child counts the number of letters in the **Consonant Family** and you write the number 21 at the side with a circle round it.

At this point you should print the word "Alphabet" as a heading and underneath print all the capital letters, making sure the child recognises them, and repeating them until he does. Afterwards, you can print each in small letters underneath the corresponding capital letter.

Compare the size of the families and talk about the little vowel family. How hard the vowels work, making words, because no words can be made without them. They are there in every word we see etc. **The child is now ready to proceed to the rest of Stage 5.**

Here, for the first time, the child is going to learn words with two vowels in them. Write down the five vowels

a e i o u

Ask the child to say their **names** and their **sounds.** Small children can be told that these are five brothers and one of them is very lazy. His name is 'e'. He is also a bully and he bullies all his brothers. Write a few three-letter words down, and ask the child to say them.

mat fat hat mad

Along comes 'e' the bully and sits at the end of the word "mat". He says to his brother 'a', "say your name, say your name" and so the word becomes "mate". The child now reads "mat, mate" and learns that when lazy 'e', who does no work himself, sits at the end of a word he makes the **sound** 'a' say the **name** 'a'. The child then does this with "fat", to make "fate", "hat, hate", "mad, made".

mat	fat	hat	mad
mate	fate	hate	made

What is actually happening is that the 'e' at the end of the word changes the short sound of the first vowel (the **sound** of the vowel), to the long sound of that vowel (the **name** of the vowel).

Write down half of the words of Set 1 without the final 'e', and ask the child to read them. The child reads the first word 'mat'; then you write an 'e' at the end of the word, to make the word 'mate' (lazy 'e' comes along and sits at the end of each "word"). The child reads 'mat-mate' as you add the 'e'.

The child reads the new words without much trouble. All he has to remember is that the 'e' at the end of the word makes the **sound** 'a' say its **name** 'a', as in 'mate'.

When the remaining written words are completed in this fashion, the words comprising the second half of the first set are written on a separate piece of paper, and treated in the same manner. (Note that many of the initial sounds are not words as such, but are simply combinations of letters; as previously, this presents no problem to the child.)

Then the child reads all the words in Set 1 to you. He then proceeds in the same fashion with Sets 2, 3 and 4.

Stage 5, Set 1 a **You must not forget lazy 'e'**

mate	take	frame	pane
fate	fake	shake	cane
hate	late	snake	hake
made	make	drake	tame
same	take	stake	safe
gate	late	grave	cave
gave	date	plane	Kate
bake	blame	sake	came
wake	flame	lame	brake

Stage 5, Set 2 i **You must not forget lazy 'e'**

ripe	while	size
kite	smile	five
time	shine	drive
fine	white	glide
ride	stile	bike
bite	side	alive
slide	pine	hide
hide	nine	like
like	mile	spike

Stage 5, Set 3 | o | **You must not forget lazy 'e'**

rope	spoke	chose
hope	hose-pipe	smoke
hole	rose	close
pole	drove	broke
stove	bone	slope
doze	poke	home
alone	stole	tone
stone	store	grove
choke	nose	wove

Stage 5, Set 4 | u | **you must not forget lazy 'e'**

tune	amuse	fume
cube	tube	tune
use	mute	cube

When working through the above Sets, this rule is very easy for the child to remember, but strangely enough, for some time in his early reading of books, he has to be reminded about "lazy e". Eventually this is not necessary.

An extra table has been introduced below (Set 5), to help the child with the rule. For example, the child has learned the word "tame" but in a reading situation, because the word he meets is "tames" or "tamed", he may be confused because the "e" is not at the end of the word; to avoid this confusion the words below should be learned. This Set is based on words from Set 1. If the child does not cope easily with Set 5 below, you should make three more similar Sets based on words from Sets 2, 3 and 4.

Stage 5, Set 5 (Set 1 plus end consonant)

mate	take	flame	stake	pane
mates	takes	flames	stakes	panes
frame	fake	flake	plane	cane
frames	fakes	flakes	planes	canes
framed	faked	flaked	planed	caned
snake	take	shake	grave	hake
snakes	takes	shakes	graves	hakes
cake	date	shake	sake	cave
cakes	dates	shakes	sakes	caves
bake	blame	tape	name	tame
bakes	blames	tapes	names	tames
baked	blamed	taped	named	tamed
wake	drake	pave	spade	hate
wakes	drakes	paves	spades	hates

Revision of Stage 5 follows. Then there is a General Revision of Stages 1 to 5. The child may not go to Stage 6 until he passes the General Revision. If a rule is forgotten he must go back, look it up and learn it again.

Stage 5 Revision. Sets 1–5

take	late	games	pine
kites	rides	hope	made
bone	ripe	bites	came
names	dome	mile	safes
liked	hole	same	plate
nine	tile	time	whine
bite	hides	ropes	smoked
stole	side	slide	skate
wake	fame	sloped	blame
canes	fate	spade	shake

General Revision: Stages 1–5

string	stamp	name	slide
crash	shelf	has	grant
loss	shall	vine	white
crush	kite	vim	mate
brick	mend	wink	whim
jump	sprat	hilt	mat
burst	pine	plate	stitch
drank	dip	van	sun
ripe	stuck	that	snake
lamp	patch	strut	punt
fetch	dug	flake	frank
toss	snake	fad	trap
hide	frisk	which	blame
shrank	mile	tape	tramp
chink	strong	ink	think
splash	stole	grin	thick

STAGE 6

Write the two vowels "ea" in a box on a sheet of paper and explain that, for the first time, two vowels in the middle of a word are going to be learned. Put a little rhyme under the vowels and ask the child to say it, making sure that he pronounces the **names** of the vowels, not their sounds:-

ea

When "e" and "a" go walking
"e" does **all** the talking.
So, what does "a" say? **NOTHING**

Now the child can attempt Set 1. Throughout Stage 6, the child has just to remember the little rhyme for each set, except for Sets 6, 9 and 10.

In Set 6 he is taught that every time he sees "y" he says "i" so the rule is y = i. In Set 9 he is taught that when "o" and "o" come together , they can make the sound "oo" as in "moon". In Set 10 he is taught that these two letters can also make the sound "oo" as in "took".

Revision follows. The child says the words as before.

Note

Spelling and **cursive (joined-up) handwriting** are started at this stage. See Appendices 1 and 2, respectively. If you decide to pursue the optional **language development programme** contained in the 'English Workbooks' recommended in Appendix 5, start it at this stage. Additional time is required for this programme – it should not use time allocated to the main reading programme.

Stage 6, Set 1 **ea**

When 'e' and 'a' go walking, 'e' does **all** the talking.

tea	beans	heap	sea
meat	speak	read	reap
meal	sea	steam	teak
eat	each	cream	weak
leaf	peach	cheap	leap
dream	treat	peas	stream
reach	teach	seat	yeast
feast	beast	least	please
fear	near	tear	hear
year	ears	mean	weave

Stage 6, Set 2 **ee**

When 'e' and 'e' go walking, the first 'e' does **all** the talking.

see	green	feed	steel
tree	keep	cheek	heel
peel	meet	wheel	week
three	sheep	sweet	sheet
creep	sleep	peep	deep
sweep	weep	sheet	seed
street	seek	wee	feet
free	need	teeth	queen
beef	seem	seen	queer

Stage 6, Set 3 **ai**

When 'a' and 'i' go walking, 'a' does **all** the talking.

rain	pail	wait	chain
train	hail	aim	sail
stain	mail	tail	nail
sail	again	vain	paid
plain	strain	gain	grain
rain	wail	laid	fail

Stage 6, Set 4 **ay**

When 'a' and 'y' go walking, 'a' does **all** the talking.

pay	say	day	May
gay	clay	away	play
stray	pray	fray	ray
jay	bay	hay	tray
way	lay	stay	may

Stage 6, Set 5 **ie**

When 'i' and 'e' go walking, 'i' does **all** the talking.

pie	lie	cries	tied
tie	die	flies	dried
pies		untied	skies
dries	spies	lied	died
	shies	pie-dish	tie-pin

Stage 6, Set 6 **y = i as in "my"**

fly	shy	dry	spy
my	why	fly	spying
crying	sky	trying	pry
why	reply	crying	sty
by	fry	frying	lying

Stage 6, Set 7 | **oa** |

When 'o' and 'a' go walking, 'o' does **all** the talking.

boat	soap	coat	load
loaf	road	float	goat
throat	toad	groan	toast
coach	roast	coast	moan
roam	whoa	coal	foal

Stage 6, Set 8 | **oe** |

When 'o' and 'e' go walking, 'o' does **all** the talking.

hoe	toe	goes	foe
woe	toes	Joe	foes
woes			

Stage 6, Set 9 | **oo** | **as in "moon"**

moon	spoon	root	roof
soon	tool	pool	cool
room	mood	shoot	roots
food	troop	droop	stoop
broom	gloom	hoof	moo
coo	too	toot	proof

Stage 6, Set 10 | **oo** | **as in "took"**

took	cook	hook	shook
nook	book	cooks	good
brook	looks	rook	hood
stood	wood	woods	rooks

Stage 6 Revision. Sets 1–10

tea	cook	seed	why
green	queen	moon	seek
again	vain	chain	train
leaf	cream	reply	room
pay	flies	goat	may
lied	teeth	stream	crook
teach	wood	hay	deep
frying	shies	shies	try
moan	yeast	crying	food
beast	hoof	sheet	grain
goes	cries	hoof	asleep
hoof	proof	wheel	foal
read	stray	please	toes
crook	laid	look	ray
away	seen	pray	trying
grain	droop	pies	weep

STAGE 7

This stage is quite straight-forward. Show the child, on a sheet of paper, the five vowels followed by the letter "r" and is asked him to sound them. This is very easy for him now at this stage:-

ar **er** **ir** **or** **ur**

At the beginning of each Set give him the guiding word shown at the top of the Set. The Sets are followed by revision. This is followed by the General Revision for Stages 6 and 7.

Stage 7, Set 1 **ar** as in "car"

car	arm	market	yard
cart	farm	carpet	card
harm	farmer	dark	hard
star	tart	charm	sharp
part	far	barn	park
pardon	smart	mark	bar
art	lark	tar	bark

Stage 7, Set 2 **er** as in "fern"

fern	November	butter	summer
term	September	lantern	porter
jerk	December	mermaid	butter
helper	October	caterpillar	butterfly
perch	perhaps	herd	cracker
her	berth	winter	Bert
sermon	helter-skelter	miller	herself
farmer	shelter	master	sister

Stage 7, Set 3 **ir** as in "bird"

bird	squirt	firm	stir	whirl	shirt
third	dirt	girl	birthday	fir-tree	squirting
skirt	first	birth	sir	twirl	swirted

Stage 7, Set 4 **or** as in "fork"

fork	cord	form	ford
sort	acorn	cork	short
horn	fort	York	storm
lord	sport	pork	form
north	worn	port	lord
shorn	storm	thorn	for

Stage 7, Set 5 | ur | as in "turn"

turn	curl	hurt	turning
burn	fur	Saturday	purr
burning	curd	churns	purse
furled	purse	burnt	nurse
burr	surf	burden	return
cur	churns	Thursday	curls

Stage 7 Revision. Sets 1–5

October	storm	December	art
first	burden	lantern	pardon
north	charm	bark	mermaid
purse	cracker	third	shirt
market	thirsty	form	fort
butter	lord	Thursday	burn
dirt	dark	carpet	September
sport	butterfly	summer	fur
turned	November	girl	stir
perhaps	twirl	thorn	pork
whirl	York	burden	master
acorn	nurse	park	porter

General Revision: Stages 6–7

meat	goes	market	away
again	farmer	need	spoon
green	broom	October	mark
say	mermaid	curl	paid
teach	birthday	burden	lantern
skies	hook	squirted	winter
weep	December	charm	girl
tray	vain	pool	mood
beast	play	queen	term
reply	sweet	wait	jay
roam	bark	first	gloom
please	porter	grain	perch
way	proof	worn	strain
queen	twirl	sheet	crook
foal	teeth	cool	sweep
weave	hay	again	stray
cream	book	seed	week

STAGE 8

For Set 1 tell the child that the sound of 'ue' is the same as the sound of 'ew', as in the little word "new". For Set 2, tell him that the sound of 'au' is the same as the sound of 'aw', as in the word "saw". In Stage 8, Sets 1–16, sounds are learned in this manner, referring to the guiding words. You explain the sounds to the child at the beginning of each set.

A little rule has to be learnt for Set 7. Write on a sheet of paper:-

When 'g' and 'e' go for a walk 'g' sounds 'j', so, ge = j

Another rule for Set 8:-

When 'c' and 'e' go for a walk 'c' sounds 's', so, ce = s

Sets 9, 10 and 11 provide the sound and the guiding word.

Stage 8, Set 1 ew = ue → new

chew	flew	threw	blue
grew	crew	blew	Sue
drew	new	pew	glue
yew	stew	news	clue
newt	dew	few	due
news-reel	brew	stew-pan	hue-and-cry

Stage 8, Set 2 aw = au → saw

lawn	crawl	dawn	Paul
saw	shawl	yawn	haul
paw	draw	raw	Saul
claw	hawk	law	fault
claws	yawns	crawling	fraud

Stage 8, Set 3 all → ball

wall	stall	fall	smaller
all	calling	fallen	smallest
ball	tall	called	taller
call	small	hall	tallest

Stage 8, Set 4 ow → owl

down	flowers	frown	allow
owl	showers	town	scowl
crown	tower	gown	bow
brown	fowls	cow	bowing

Stage 8, Set 5 ou → out

our	pout	mouse	hound
out	found	house	cloud
sour	round	bound	proud
loud	mouth	sound	pout

Stage 8, Set 6 oi = oy → oil, boy

soil	coil	coin	Joy
oil	boil	moist	enjoy
toil	foil	point	joyful
joint	boiling	soiling	employ
noise	spoil	join	toys
toiling	spoiling	joining	boy
pointing	boiled	royal	annoy

Stage 8, Set 7 ge = j as in age

When 'g' and 'e' go together 'ge' says 'j'

page	stage	large	ledge
cage	edge	bridge	ridge
rage	judge	badge	nudge
huge	wage	wedge	lodge
germ	orange	badge	smudge
German	Germany	sledge	hedge
strange	stranger	urge	manger

Stage 8, Set 8 ce = s as in nice

When 'c' and 'e' go together 'ce' says 's'

nice	grace	price	peace
price	pence	voice	place
lace	rice	mice	trace
slice	ice	race	choice
twice	face	ice-cream	produce
trace	space	dice	trace

Stage 8, Set 9 y as in happy

happy		chilly	bunny
sunny	dolly	mummy	granny
copy	empty	forty	Jimmy
dolly	fifty	Billy	Fanny
scrappy	lumpy	sadly	rainy
nanny	gladly	pity	puppy
candy	curly	stormy	Kitty
marry	sorry	carry	sherry
merry	tarry	ferry	scurry
berry	Harry	hurry	lorry

Stage 8, Set 10 **ey** **as in turkey**

kidney	chimney	jockey	Charley
jersey	valley	jersey	donkey

Stage 8, Set 11 **le** **as in apple**

twinkle	tangle	kettle	crumple
little	bangle	needle	muddle
steeple	single	thimble	apples
tumble	battle	bottle	middle
eagle	nibble	bubble	candle
cackle	settle	jingle	scramble

Stage 8 can present difficulties to the child, and if this is the case, before going on to the revision words it is recommended to carry out the reinforcement technique described in Stage 2 Revision, modified slightly as in the following two paragraphs.

If this is required, prepare paper squares, (2" x 2"), and write out all the new sounds from Stage 8, e.g. ew, aw, ow, ou, etc. in **large print,** without the helping word, one sound per square. Make a game of learning these sounds in a similar way to the random testing used in the "Look, Say and Remember" approach. Spread the squares out face down; the child lifts them up one at a time and gives the correct sound.

If any of the sounds have been forgotten, go back to the appropriate set or sets and repeat them until the child can read the words easily. Do another random test until the child gets **every** sound right.

When the child passes the following revision he gets the sheets of words which make up Stage 8 to put into his folder.

Stage 8 Revision. Sets 1–11

crew	flower	fifty	crawling
lawn	round	carry	fallen
fallen	moist	valley	scowl
crown	large	tangle	clown
hound	price	due	pointed
employ	sadly	crawl	wage
stage	ferry	smallest	nice
wedge	donkey	gown	chilly
rice	thimble	proud	yawn
happy	glue	employ	royal
twinkle	fraud	smudge	kettle
jersey	stall	produce	newt
few	mouse	stormy	sour
hawk	joining	bubble	bridge
fault	hedge	nibble	choice
small	peace	stew	lorry

STAGE 9

This is the last of the main stages. It deals with silent letters. Each set has its own little rule which has to be learnt.

Set 1 introduces silent 'gh'. Write the two letters in a box on a sheet of paper. Tell child that when 'g' and 'h' are in the middle of a word they go to sleep, for example silent 'gh' as in light.

Stage 9, Set 1 silent 'gh' light

When 'g' and 'h' are in the middle they go to sleep.

might	bright	tight	fighting
sigh	right	flight	night
fight	light	alight	sight
high	highest	mighty	brightest
higher	fighter	tighter	lighter

Stage 9, Set 2 silent 'k' knot

The child learns that 'k' can go to sleep.

knot	know	known	knew
knack	knee	kneel	knelt
knead	knife	knob	knave
knock	knit	knell	knight

Stage 9, Set 3 silent 'b' numb

The child learns that 'b' can go to sleep.

limb	plumb	plumber	debt
lamb	crumb	dumb	debtor
jamb	numb	thumb	debts
doubt	climb	comb	combing

Stage 9, Set 4 silent 'w' wrap

The child learns that 'w' can go to sleep.

wrap	wreck	wrist	wring
wren	whole	wrench	wreath
write	wrote	wretch	wrestle
wrong	writer	wrung	sword

Stage 9, Set 5 silent 't' often

The child learns that when 't' is in the middle of a word, he can go to sleep.

often	soften	bristle	bustle
gristle	hustle	nestle	fastened
whistle	wrestle	thistle	glisten
castle	rustle	listened	bristles

Stage 9, Set 6 silent 'l' half

The child learns that when 'l' is in the middle of a word, he can go to sleep.

half	calf	palm	chalk
stalk	walk	calm	talk
balm	folk	walking	talker

Stage 9, Set 7 silent 'g' gnat

The child learns that 'g' can go to sleep.

gnat	gnu	gnaw	campaign
gnarled	gnome	gnashed	deign
gnawing	gnash	sign	reign

Stage 9 Revision. Sets 1–7

sign	higher	stalk	knew
knock	palm	reign	debtor
numb	campaign	highest	wrote
wring	lighter	knife	hustle
whistle	knife	debts	calm
folk	comb	writer	gnarled
sign	wreath	wrestle	brightest
talking	fastened	half	knee
alight	deign	mighty	wrong
knight	soften	knitted	gristle
plumber	flight	doubt	calming
wretch	knave	wreck	gnashing
often	combing	calf	brighter
balm	wrench	signed	known
gnaw	castle	sigh	doubting
gnash	chalk	gnome	thumb

General Revision: Stages 1–9

cuff	tubes	chain	sigh
sulk	which	gnome	broth
fuss	bench	shelter	while
mint	dream	manger	twirl
pond	strain	smudge	shall
whiskers	highest	rustle	style
more	stuff	those	shrank
punt	please	thirty	perch
ashore	queen	campaign	trash
valid	astray	rock	wrong
care	edge	victim	stretch
yelp	pleasing	deign	glint
spikes	flinch	mighty	vagabond
prepare	palm	gnat	crock
cubes	moss	knife	known
newt	tease	leaves	tune
frown	silk	tunes	frame
produce	stalk	signed	speck
sledge	away	slight	snatch
dust	quite	store	chalk

Additional Phonic Tables

A few remaining examples have been selected to "round off" the child's phonetic experience; many are exceptions to the rules previously learned. In some of these eighteen sets only a few words have been given. You can increase these with the help of a dictionary.

1. After the consonants 'd' and 't' the suffix "ed" forms an additional syllable, i.e. both final letters are sounded.

aided	pointed	stated	patted
shouted	jointed	roasted	blotted
batted	fated	handed	tested
tasted	plated	dotted	stunted

2. After the consonants 'c', 'ck', 'k', 'f', 'pp', 'ph', 'ss', 'sh', 'x,' 'ch', the suffix "ed" is sounded 't', i.e. the 'e' is silent. For example the word "jumped" is sounded "jumpt", and "milked" is sounded "milkt".

jumped	backed	faced	roofed	rapped
taxed	dropped	tossed	pushed	autographed
hatched	creaked	milked	priced	liked

3. In nearly all words not covered by tables 1 and 2, "ed" is pronounced 'd'.

tumbled	mailed	turned	jarred	killed
tattered	moved	drowned	stayed	spilled
seized	showed	called	crumpled	sailed

4. Usually the vowel followed by one consonant is long; when the consonant is doubled the vowel is usually short.

biter	diner	doted	hoping	holy
bitter	dinner	dotted	hopping	holly

hater	riding	caning	planing	robed
hatter	ridding	canning	planning	robbed

5. In the following words the final 'e' does not lengthen the preceding vowel.

have	office	shone	favourite
give	service	gone	granite
active	notice	medicine	festive
native	lattice	engine	expensive

6. In the following table "ow" has the **long sound** of "o"

crow	blow	sow	below	arrow
crowed	blows	sowed	snow	own
crowing	blowing	sowing	window	mow
show	bowl	flow	grow	mowing
showed	bowled	flown	grown	mowed
showing	bowling	flowing	growing	slow

7. In the following words "o" and "ou" have the **short sound** of "u".

mother	honey	country
comfort	London	honey
money	some	couple
love	Monday	cousin

8. In the following words "o" and "ou" have the **long sound** of "o".

old	told	gold	rolled	sold
bolt	cold	bold	fold	hold
stroll	ago	scold	most	droll
mould	shoulder	soul	moult	boulder
bold	post	host	roller	colder
colt	jolt	posy	soda	toll

9. In the following words "ear" sounds "air".

bear	pear	swear	tear	wear

10. In the following words "ear" sounds "ur".

pearl	earth	heard	learn	search

11. In the following words "or" sounds "ur".

work	worm	worth	world	worst

12. In the following words "i" has the **long sound.**

find	rind	behind	child	tiny
mind	blind	tiger	wild	kind

13. In the following words "ea" has the **short sound** of "e".

bread	dead	head	spread	meant
breadth	tread	stead	lead	dread
health	wealth	instead	death	read
healthy	wealthy	steady	deaf	ready

14. A few examples of final "y" changed to "ie" before "s" or "d".

try	pity	copy	tidy	carry
tries	pities	copies	tidies	carries
tried	pitied	copied	tidied	carried

15. In the following words "ie" and "ei" have the **long sound** of "e".

field	priest	seize	fiend	wield
grief	yield	ceiling	piece	shield
brief	chief	receive	thief	relief
grieve	belief	receipt	frieze	believe
niece	siege	deceive	shriek	thieves

16. In the following words "ph" is sounded like "f".

photograph	telephone	paragraph
phlox	nephew	triumph
physics	orphan	symphony
phrase	pamphlet	dolphin

17. In the following words two vowels together are sounded separately.

fuel	giant	trial	diet	dual
poet	radio	cruel	piano	lion

18. In the following words "tion" and "sion" are pronounced "shun".

nation	admission	pension	protection
fraction	omission	mission	extension
affection	addition	subtraction	invention

Chapter 3
Teaching Programme for the Older Child

If a child of 9 years or older is not reading fluently, emotional problems based on frustration usually arise, and are revealed in a variety of ways in his behaviour. Often he is either aggressive or becomes completely withdrawn. The bright, cheerful child who began school at the age of 5 years becomes disillusioned, angry and unhappy.

Obviously, the older child has had a major setback in learning the most important subject in his school life. The child has lost everything, which in turn makes him feel inferior or stupid. The more sensitive he is, the more emotional the situation becomes. Some children are so upset that they cannot look at books and refuse all help. They have lost all confidence. It's as if they had built a brick wall around themselves that no one can break down.

The approach to break down the emotional barrier must be one that immediately gives the child success and hope. At eight years and above most children are mentally ready for Part 3, Phonics Course, which is the fastest method of acquiring the skill of reading. The teaching approach with the older child follows a different sequence. If not already known, single sounds are learnt. To build confidence with rapid success, phonic development follows, and, to maintain interest "Look, Say and Remember" is introduced at the end of Stage 5 of the Phonic Course. **Do not introduce books until after Stage 5 of the Phonic Course.**

Note that these principles apply also to Secondary school children and adults. Because the recommended books have good word repetition and gradation they are also suitable for older children and adults. In the early, mechanical stages of learning to read, the child or adult is more interested in getting words correct than in the subject matter, which is of secondary importance. In one-to-one lessons there is no need for embarrassment.

Single Sounds

The first step is to ensure that the child knows all the single sounds. If he does not know them they must be taught, using the method described in Chapter 2.

Phonic Development

When single sounds are mastered, proceed with the Phonic Course in Part 3 of Chapter 2, following every step carefully.

Note that with the older child the letter-size shown in the Phonics Course is required only for the first two sets of Stage 1. After this the letters can be the same size as in the first "Look, Say and Remember" book. Also, from the beginning the older child will use style (a) on page 16 for word formation.

When the child has reached Set 5 in Stage 1 of the Phonics Course, 141 words have been made and read. This is a great incentive to continue, and he will begin to enjoy making and saying words. He now realises that this technique helps him to read words and will be trying for the first 500 words, and so on. Soon he will become completely absorbed in the stages to follow.

Only leave Stage 1 of the Phonic Course when you are sure the child is coping well with the three-letter words. The child is told that the length of the words is not important at this stage; the important thing is that he has discovered that he can read words by applying the rules. He is told that he will be able to sound longer words in the same way, once he has learned more rules.

Look, Say and Remember

On completion of Stage 5 of the Phonic Course, the child is introduced to the "Look, Say and Remember" technique. He will be able to cope with this while continuing with his phonic work. Just follow the procedure in Chapter 2.

The series of books "One, Two, Three and Away!" is not used for the older child; the starting point for "Look, Say and Remember" in this case is the first book in the Beacon Readers series (see Appendix 5). I call the early volumes 'fun books'. Contrary to general opinion, older children do not find these early books childish. I have used these books over the years with Secondary school children of eleven years and above. Their reaction was joy that they could read words and stories that they could not read before.

As more and more phonic rules are taught alongside the "Look, Say and Remember" technique it is noticeable how the child's reading pattern changes. No longer has he to be told words that he can work out for himself. The noting of unknown words decreases until it is almost negligible. The phonic rules begin to predominate and less and less "Look, Say and Remember" words have to be given.

Spelling

Spelling can be introduced on completion of the "Look, Say and Remember" work in the second book of the Beacon series. Carry out the procedures detailed in Appendix 1, and note that the use of the kinesthetic method produces early success with words from the child's own verbal vocabulary.

Language Development

When the "Look, Say and Remember" work has reached the end of the fourth book of the Beacon series, the use of the 'English Workbooks' recommended in Appendix 5 can begin. Older children start with Book 1, not the two Introductory Books.

Handwriting

Development of cursive handwriting can begin at the same time as language development. Carry out the procedures in Appendix 2.

Conclusion

Commitment to the so-essential daily routine is the key to success. Not only will your child establish himself as a fluent reader but his school work will improve tremendously; also, the change in his behaviour will be most noticeable. Older children who have learned to read become avid readers once they have finished with the mechanics of reading. Parents find real joy in discovering that they are hard-pressed to keep them going in books.

Chapter 4
Teaching the Dyslexic Child to Read

Dyslexia: this rare complaint was first recognised in America in 1872 and in Britain in the 1890's. During the 1920's more research was carried out, and mental pathologists named the condition "word-blindness" or alexia (inability to read). They believed the condition to be due to a congenital brain defect and to be hopelessly incurable, so they lost all interest in it.

Dr Grace Fernald thought otherwise; her firm belief was that a person of normal intelligence could learn all the basic skills. She carried out experimental work with children said to be in this category, at the University of California in Los Angeles. These children were not responding to the teaching of reading by the conventional methods of that time.

She was the first to demonstrate beyond all doubt that the most extreme cases of "word blindness" were quickly and completely curable. Her "cures" were proclaimed, not only in America, but in many countries throughout the world. "Cured" pupils were not only able to take part in normal school life but, as her records show, they went on to universities, colleges and to different careers requiring high academic achievement.

According to Schonell in 'The Psychology and Teaching of Reading', "photographs of the eyes during reading show that the process consists of a series of eye movements and eye pauses. Nothing is read while the eyes are in motion but only during the momentary pauses."

There is a small proportion of children whose eye movements do not mature with the rest of their mental and physical development. It appears that the child might see the first and last letter of the word and then go back in eye movement to the middle of the word. He becomes utterly confused and reading becomes impossible.

The child who suffers from this disability is said to be dyslexic. It occurs with children of all abilities, but it cannot be too strongly stressed that the number of children with this condition is very small. Many excellent teachers have taught reading successfully throughout their whole careers without meeting such a child.

Non-Dyslexic Difficulties

There are conditions often confused with dyslexia that can be remedied in a simple manner. These are dealt with here, before describing the programme for dyslexic children.

Children who confuse the names and sounds of certain letters and read small words wrongly are not necessarily dyslexic. The most common letter confusions are "b, p, d," "m, n" and "c, e". The most common word confusions are "on and no" and "saw and was".

To overcome the confusion with single letters, write two or three of the letters that are causing difficulty at the top of a sheet of paper, for example "b", "p", "d". Put a triangle, circle and square, respectively, round these three letters. Now write each of these three letters ten or twelve times in random positions on the sheet of paper. Ask the child to put the appropriate symbol (triangle, circle or square) around each of the letters in turn, saying its name and sound as he does so. He may need to do several sheets in this fashion; be patient, the confusion does vanish. The same procedure can be adopted for "m" and "n", or any other two letters that the child confuses.

In the case of confusion with small words, ask the child to point to the first letter of the word. As he points he must sound this letter several times, finally saying the word correctly. Constant repetition of this procedure will cause this fault to disappear gradually.

Be aware that dyslexia is not fully understood, and test methods are imprecise. Before using the following procedures for dyslexic children, try the standard system in this book, which has worked for many children who were incorrectly diagnosed as being dyslexic.

Method used by Dr Grace Fernald to help dyslexic children

The materials and equipment required are plain sheets of paper 12" x 4" and 8" x 2", filing boxes for each size of paper, a thick, black-felt-tip pen, and access to a typewriter.

In developing her method for treating this disability Dr. Fernald concentrated on the theory of eye movement noted above. Her programme was based on an approach relying initially on vision, hearing and touch, with the emphasis on hearing and touch. It is known as the kinesthetic method. The earliest written records of this approach date from around 400 B.C. and various forms of this teaching have come down through the centuries to the present day. Most dyslexic children can benefit from this programme from the age of seven. Seeing, hearing and touch gives way to seeing and hearing. No phonic rules are used and the method is inevitably slower than the normal teaching procedures used in this book.

Step 1

At the beginning the child is told that there is a new way of learning words, which he could try. He is told that many people have had the same difficulty as himself in learning to read. These people have learned easily by this new way which is as good as any other.

The child is asked which word he would like to be able to read. The word is written out on one of the 12" x 4" strips of paper using a thick, black-felt-tip pen in **cursive ("joined-up")** writing, for example:-

television

To show the procedure to the child, the parent traces the word with her index finger, using the same hand with which the child writes. As the parent traces she says the word aloud, "tel-e-vision". She should be at the end of the word when she finishes sounding it.

The child then does this several times, tracing the word with finger contact, using the index finger of the hand with which he writes, saying the word aloud as he traces, and completing the tracing and sounding of the word simultaneously.

The strip is then turned over and the child attempts to write the word on a separate sheet of paper. The child will not use cursive writing, unless he has already been taught to write in this way; he will probably print the letters, but the "style" is unimportant for this technique. He may get it correct straight away or he may get only as far as "tele", for example. If he cannot complete the word, he turns the strip over, looks at the word, and begins again to trace it, saying it aloud. **Each try that has been written and not completed must be scored out. The word must be written afresh until it is written correctly.**

He may do several words in this fashion at the first session. The next day he is shown these four or five words, **typewritten.** He is able to read them. This is a tremendous breakthrough for the child.

When pronouncing words for the child, care must be taken to say short words just as they are spoken. There must not be a distorted, stilted sounding-out of the letters or syllables, because the word-sound can be lost. For example, the word "trust" is said as a whole, **not** tr-u-s-t. The sound for each letter is never given separately or over-emphasised. However, longer words can be broken up while tracing, such as "in-div-id-ual". To summarize, short words are traced as a whole while longer words are broken up into their natural division. Tracing and sounding must end at the same time.

When the child has discovered that he **can** learn to write words, he begins "story writing". At first he writes about anything that interests him. At this stage the stories are very short, perhaps only three sentences. As his skill increases, his stories become longer.

He asks for any word he does not know how to write. Each word is written for him and learned by him as previously, before it is written in his story. It has been known, in some cases, that the child has had to trace every word in his story. He may have to trace some of the words many times. Whatever he writes is **typed for him within 24 hours** so that he may read the printed form the next day.

Step 2

After a period of tracing, the child is able to learn any new word by simply looking at the word in cursive writing, saying it over to himself, or aloud as he looks at it, then writing it without looking at the copy, saying each part of the word as he writes it. Writing and sounding the word must end at the same time.

Learning words without tracing is a gradual process. At one session the child may need to trace every new word. At another, perhaps two words are traced and three or four words are learned by looking at the word and saying it. When he definitely does not need to trace he is ready for Step 3.

In the child's story-writing his own vocabulary should be used. It is better for him to start with words he already knows in his speech. Development of his spoken vocabulary is a continuing process and can be greatly enhanced by parents talking or reading to him, using a variety of words which will expand his vocabulary.

As the work with the child proceeds he learns to file all his "words" in alphabetical order. This can be done by using a box-file (which could be a shoe-box). This box-file contains white cardboard strips; each strip has a letter of the alphabet printed on it. The child will be slow initially to identify the first letter of the word with the same letter in the file. After some practice he will become quite skilful at this, and will really enjoy putting the "words" in the correct place.

In this manner the alphabet is learnt without rote learning and without too much emphasis on letters in words. The child learns all the letters of the alphabet, which, in turn, is paving the way for the use of a dictionary.

Step 3

When the child asks for a word it is now **printed** (not cursive writing) by hand on a smaller sheet (8" x 2") with a black-felt-tip pen. The word must not be printed too small; the whole of the strip should be used. He looks at the word, says it, writes it, and then transfers it to his story. Finally he puts the strip of paper with the word on it in a small box-file in alphabetical order. Just as the large box-file had to accommodate a 12" long strip of paper, so the small box should accommodate an 8" paper strip.

By this time many stories have been written, initially with just a few sentences in each one, but gradually getting longer and longer. The child now reaches the stage when he wants to read from books.

Step 4

Here the child is introduced to books. Care must be taken that these first books are not too difficult. Words from the many new stories he has written and learnt and seen in print will now stand him in good stead. As he is reading he is told words he does not know and he continues reading, thus keeping the reading fluent. When the reading is finished the new words are printed by the parent on strips of paper as in Step 3. The child looks at each word, says it and writes it. Later, these words must be checked to make sure they are known and have become a part of the reading vocabulary. The checking techniques described in the section "Look, Say and Remember" in Chapter 2 are used.

Step 5

By now the child has the ability to recognise new words from their similarity to words or parts of words he has learnt before.

He is eager to read, and is allowed to read as much as he wants, about anything in which he is interested. He is coping with new words, often from their resemblance to words he already knows. He must not be read to during this period; he must read for himself.

Lastly, before reading to an adult, he is asked to look over a paragraph or page and lightly underline any words that are new. He is now able to pick these out quite quickly. These are printed as usual for him and are presented to him and checked as described in Step 4. The child is told the meaning of any word he does not know already. He then reads the paragraph or page to the adult successfully.

According to Dr. Fernald the retention of words learnt in this way is 88 to 95 percent. By the time the child no longer requires help with words in print and is reading fluently, he is ready to develop his reading skills without this type of help. He will go from strength to strength and his reading difficulties will have vanished.

Appendix 1
Spelling Course

Spelling sessions can begin as soon as the child has completed Stage 5 of the Phonic Course.

If the first attempt at spelling proves to be too much, too soon, it is much better to leave it for the time being and continue with the phonic sets. Later, perhaps at Stage 6 or at your own discretion, try a few words again. At no time must there be any pressure on the child to spell the words. He will do it when he is ready. Children love to "show off" when they can spell, and enjoy their spelling lessons when they are ready for them.

The First Week

Words that the child has already learnt to "sound and say" are the starting point, beginning at Stage 1, Set 1 of the phonic work in this book. Use the sheets of words that have been "won" so far during the Phonic Course

Initially you may find that the child can spell the three-letter words in Stage 1 orally, (Steps 1 and 2 below), without having to write them. If this does occur, continue with the oral spelling until the child hesitates over a word which he is unable to spell. This determines the starting point of the written spelling technique (Step 3 below). After the written learning technique is begun, each lesson follows the four-step programme described below.

For the first week, six words are selected from Set 1. On Monday the child learns the first three words, on Tuesday the second three words, on Wednesday the odd words (1, 3, & 5), and on Thursday the even words (2, 4, & 6). On Friday test work is carried out to determine if the child can spell the six words.

Step 1. Print the first three words from Set 1 of Stage 1 of the phonic work on a sheet of paper as follows:-

sat
sap
Sam

Step 2. The child looks at the first word and spells it by saying the **name** of each letter, followed by saying the word:-

'ess' 'ai' 'tee' → sat

He repeats this several times, looking at the word. Turn the paper over and asks the child to spell the word 'sat'.

Usually this presents no problem as the word is already part of his reading vocabulary from the earlier phonic work. If necessary, repeat Steps 1 and 2 until the child can spell the word correctly.

Step 3. The child learns the three words in this manner. Then give him a sheet of paper and a pencil. Say the words one at a time; the child writes them down. In doing this it is helpful to put the words in a meaningful sentence, as illustrated in the following procedure:-

a. Say the word that the child has to write, e.g. 'sat'.

b. Make up and say a short sentence containing the word, e.g. 'The boy **sat** on a chair', stressing the word 'sat'.

c. Say the word 'sat' again; then the child writes the word.

This technique should be used throughout the spelling programme. It is especially useful for longer words or words which are pronounced alike but have different meanings, e.g. 'made' and 'maid'.

Step 4. If a mistake does occur in any word, the child goes back to the original sheet (Step 1) and learns the word again. In the early stages there is often no need to re-learn the words.

Testing and revision is carried out on Fridays. Call out the six words, in the manner already suggested (Step 3), going at the child's pace of writing. Any mistake must be corrected and revised until the child writes the word correctly. When he has successfully spelt the words the child writes them in an exercise book kept only for spelling lessons.

Subsequent Weeks

After the first week, add either one or two words per week to the word list, depending on the performance of the child; don't exceed twenty words per week. Note that spelling skills vary widely among children, and **the learning process should proceed at the pace of the child.**

Continue this procedure with the words in the first five sets of Stage 1 of the phonic programme; it is not necessary for the child to spell the words in Sets 6 to 14 of Stage 1. Then proceed with the words in Stage 2 of the phonic programme and follow this with the remaining stages until all the words in the first nine stages have been spelt correctly.

Then introduce the child to 'The Essential Spelling List' by Fred Schonell, mentioned in the Book List. This is an excellent book which caters for children up to the age of twelve years. Eight new words are introduced at a time; in all there are 3,200 words. Many of the words that the child meets in the phonic work and the "Look, Say and Remember" work will be encountered in the early stages of this book. Follow the principles outlined above. Do oral spelling until the child hesitates over a word and cannot spell it; this is the starting point for written spelling.

The Kinesthetic Method as an Aid to Spelling

Note that children who are fluent readers sometimes find difficulty in learning to spell. The use of the kinesthetic method can help them tremendously. The spelling of longer words, from the child's own verbal vocabulary, can be learned easily, giving a sense of achievement and satisfaction to the child. Not only is this exciting for the child, but also it extends his written vocabulary.

I have used the kinesthetic method with such children, who were surprised at how easy it was to spell using this technique. What was more exciting, months later they had not forgotten how to spell words learned in this manner.

However, it is a slow method of learning to spell, and should only be used with fluent readers who are having difficulty with the standard approach to spelling.

The method is similar to that described in Chapter 4 for teaching reading to dyslexic children, but with minor modifications, as follows:-

The child selects eight words that he would like to spell. Write he first word, in **large cursive writing,** on a strip of paper 12" x 4". To show the procedure to the child, trace over the word with your index finger, using the same hand with which the child writes. As you trace you say the word aloud. You should be at the end of the word when you finish sounding it. Tell the child the meaning of the word.

The child then does this several times, tracing the word with finger contact, using the index finger of the hand with which he writes, saying the word aloud as he traces, and completing tracing and sounding of the word simultaneously.

The strip is then turned over and the child attempts to write the word on a separate sheet of paper. The child will not use cursive writing unless he has already been taught to write in this way; he will probably print the letters, but the "style" is unimportant for this technique. He may write the word correctly straight away or he may get only as far as the first three or four letters. If he cannot complete the word, he turns the strip over, looks at the word and begins to trace it, saying it aloud. **Each try that has been written and not completed must be scored out. The word must be written afresh until is written correctly.**

Care must be taken when pronouncing words for the child. **Refer to paragraph 5 on page 55 for the technique.**

When the child can spell the word correctly then he copies it into his spelling exercise book. At the end of the week there is a test on all the words that have been traced. This is a highly satisfactory experience for the child. Words he thought he would never be able to spell will be "easy".

Appendix 2
Handwriting

Learning cursive, or "joined-up", writing should be introduced at the end of Stage 5 of the phonics programme. These notes are included so that the child can get the best results from the two books recommended in Appendix 5.

These books suggest that they should be used from the age of seven; however it is not necessary to wait until this age to begin this type of writing. Most children want to write. If you think your child is capable of coping with these books, follow the instructions and "have a go". The child sets the pace and you supply the patience. Perseverance will be very rewarding to both of you, but if it is unsuccessful at the first attempt, leave it and try it again later.

Instructions about the correct way to hold a pencil, sitting properly etc. are given on the inside of the front cover of both books.

The only additional materials required are two packets of paper (approx. 12" x 8"), one unlined and the other lined, some black pencil-type crayons and some HB grade pencils.

Patterns

Using the *plain paper* and pencil-type crayons, show the child how to make the first practice pattern. To make it easier for the child, make the pattern approximately *twice the size* of the one illustrated in the book. The main purpose of the exercise at this stage is to keep the lines of the pattern straight and firm. Since the paper is unlined, no attempt can be made to keep the pattern between two ruled lines as it appears in the book.

When you are satisfied that this has been accomplished, using the whole sheet probably to prove it, tackle the second pattern. As before, make it twice as big as the one in the book. Again, the main purpose is for the child to get the slant of the pattern correct and firm; maintaining the pattern between two ruled lines is unnecessary at this stage.

Change to the HB pencil as recommended in the book. Reduce the size of the pattern to that used in the book. Still using the plain paper make sure that the child is capable of doing the first two patterns. When this is satisfactory **change to the lined paper.**

On a sheet of lined paper, copy the first pattern as illustrated in the book, getting the child to complete it to the end of the sheet. Continue doing this until you are satisfied that the child can start and stop each drawn line at the ruled lines on the sheet of paper, and can achieve the correct spacing between each drawn line. Do exactly the same for the second pattern, taking care that the distance between each slant line is similar to that in the book. When you are pleased with the child's efforts then comes the reward. The child completes the first two patterns in the book and is praised for neatness.

These instructions are spread over a period of time, going at the child's pace. Don't expect too much at the beginning; the time required to complete these patterns can vary widely from child to child.

Continue in this fashion using plain paper and pencil-type crayons, followed by lined paper, practising each pattern until you are sure that the child, as a reward, is ready to transfer his efforts neatly to the book. One pattern at a time is sufficient. Although this seems to be a slow process, it is all worth-while. As the child progresses through the other exercises in the book you will see the result of your labours.

Single Letters

Once the child has completed the ten patterns on the first page of the first book, and you are satisfied with his efforts, he is ready to try individual letters. There are three stages in Book 1 to help with the formation of each letter. Use the same technique as for the patterns. First, on unlined paper, mark out the dots as shown in the book, but in a larger size and using pencil-type crayons. Do the letter "l" for the child to trace over, and finally let the child try the letter "l" on his own.

Now, with the HB pencil, copy the three stages on lined paper, getting the child to do them as previously. When you are satisfied with the child's effort the reward comes by allowing the child to do the letter "l" in the book.

Eventually the child will only use the lined paper and pencil to practice with before he transfers his work to the book. If care is taken in the early stages, the child always practising on lined paper first, before transferring to the book, you will find that the joining-up process presents no problem whatsoever later on.

By the time the child reaches the last two pages of Book 1 a neat form of handwriting has been established. Note that on the second last page not all the letters are joined-up. These words must be copied exactly as given. On the last page all the letters are joined-up. These words must also be copied exactly as given.

This is good preparation for Book 2. Here the teaching method is the same. Copy on lined paper, and transfer to the book when the copied work is up to standard.

Appendix 3

Current Primary School Teaching Methods

The three main approaches used today in Primary Schools for the teaching of reading are 'Phonics', 'Look and Say' and 'Psycholinguistics'; they are described briefly below.

Phonics

Phonics methods are based on decoding written words through sound. The sounds of individual letters are learnt, followed by the sounds of various letter combinations. Exercises to practise the use of these sounds include the reading of word lists and short stories. In a good scheme the stories are both interesting and carefully graded for word difficulty and repetition.

Phonics programmes were universally used in this country during the first half of this century and can be termed the 'traditional' approach. Some problems can result from the inconsistencies of the English language, and a good phonics programme will address this issue; however it should not be claimed that a phonics programme alone can complete the learning of reading.

A more important issue, not commonly recognised, is that success in the use of a phonics programme depends on introducing it at the correct time in the mental development of a child. If it is introduced too early the child will not be able to cope and will become discouraged quickly.

Phonics programmes are considered 'old-fashioned' by many teacher training organisations, and consequently are now not widely used in Primary schools. Phonics are an integral part of the teaching programme in this book.

Look and Say

This technique was introduced to this country from America in the 1950's and became popular in the 1960's. It is based on the idea that children learn to read by recognising the shapes of written words. A 'sight' vocabulary is built up by repetition. A series of books, graded for word difficulty and repetition, is used to develop this vocabulary, providing interest and reinforcement of the learned words.

Compared with phonics programmes 'Look and Say' can be introduced to a child, with success, at an earlier stage in his mental development. It was introduced in schools as a replacement for phonics programmes which, when used alone, were not working for all children. To what extent this was due to the use of phonics before such children were sufficiently mentally mature cannot be known.

In many Primary schools today 'Look and Say' is not carried out rigorously. To use the technique properly each new word must be repeated until it is recognised out of context.

Cross-checking is required to ensure that the child is not "reading" the book from memory, but is actually recognising and reading each word. The technique forms a part of the teaching programme in this book, but, to emphasise the need for proper recognition of the learnt words, it is termed here "Look, Say and Remember".

Psycholinguistics

This term is used to describe techniques based on the idea that children learn to read in the same way as they learn to speak. Attractively illustrated books, with a word, phrase or sentence printed under each illustration, are used to associate words and objects. This is the theory behind 'Emergent Reading' or 'Real Books', and the 'Apprenticeship Approach', also called 'Paired Reading'. These ideas were introduced here in 1980 and became extremely popular by 1985. There is still no statistical basis for the theory, and these ideas are not used in the teaching programme in this book. Basically these techniques are planned around the 'Look and Say' method, but can be too difficult for many children because they have little or no reinforcement element to ensure that individual words are properly learnt.

Real Book Reading

In this technique the child chooses a book and the teacher reads it to him. He reads it with the teacher. He then reads it by himself and when he has finished the book he can select another one.

A danger with the technique is that the child may not be reading but simply remembering the words and repeating them "parrot fashion", without recognizing individual words.

Paired Reading

This is another variation of 'Look and Say' and could be called "telling and hearing", with an adult working with the child; it also requires no teaching and has been called the 'Apprenticeship Approach'. The procedure is broadly as follows. The child, perhaps with guidance, chooses a book to read. Then the adult and child sit together and begin reading out loud together, the adult providing a model of correct reading to the child. The child sets the pace and must pronounce all the words correctly. If the child cannot read a word, or pronounces a word incorrectly, the adult provides the correction and the child repeats it. Then both continue reading as before.

If the child wishes to read a little on his own some non-verbal signal is given e.g. a knock or nudge. During independent reading the adult gives constant praise and encouragement, especially if errors are corrected by the child. Negative help, where the adult corrects errors, is combined with positive help, praising successes.

When a child is reading independently and is stumped by a word the adult must give it and then join in again. Paired Reading then continues until the child signals to go on alone. The adult should stop periodically and talk about the book. This could be done by looking at the illustrations and discussing them, or by trying to guess what is going to happen on the next page. It could also be done by relating the story to the experiences of the child.

This procedure assumes that the child is already reading and is of little help to the non-reader. Even if the child can read a few words he is at a disadvantage to remember words in this way, because there is little reinforcement and no cross-checking to ensure that each word is known. However the method does have benefits for children already reading, in providing both encouragement and correction of errors.

As well as being used in school this method can also be carried out at home. Increasingly, parents are being encouraged to do reading with their children, but often receive inadequate guidance. Some parents found that "Paired Reading" did not work because the child was not yet reading and could not cope with this type of reading situation.

Children who have succeeded with 'Real Books' and 'Paired Reading' are often 'natural readers' who would learn to read using any method. It does not follow that 'natural readers' are all at the higher end of the I.Q. range; it appears that they are endowed with good visual, hearing and retention attributes. Unfortunately, many children are not 'natural readers' and they have to work at acquiring a high reading age. This they thoroughly enjoy when they are succeeding in a well-planned, structured approach.

Silent Reading

'Silent Reading' is part of the curriculum in many Infant and Junior Schools. Called "Uninterrupted Sustained Silent Reading", or "Everyone Reading in Class", the whole class or, often, the whole school, devotes a certain amount of time, typically thirty minutes, at a set time of day, to silent reading.

Silent reading is not intended to be a teaching technique. A recent pamphlet on the subject states that the purpose of this activity is "to show children that reading can and should be much more than just a school subject. A programme of Silent Reading provides students with the opportunity to experience reading in its most meaningful context and to see wide reading as a means to enhance their personal lives in many ways".

The child chooses a book or books he wants to read and, together with the class, reads silently while the teacher is reading her book. Silent reading assumes that the child is able to read, and provides encouragement to children to develop their own interests, but there is no liaison between teacher and pupil if the pupil comes across a word he cannot read.

Whilst clearly desirable for those who can read, other children can find this time almost unbearable as they cannot yet read; they can only look at the pictures.

Appendix 4

Back to Basics

The Lost Years

The teaching methods used in schools are influenced by teacher training colleges and local area-advisers and inspectors and the latter can have significant influence over the careers of teachers. All these groups obtain ideas and information on methods from university researchers, develop their policies and pass them on to the schools. In the case of reading, the weak link in this sequence is that the university researchers are not very certain about the way(s) in which children learn to read. Critics have said that, in order to maintain credibility as sources of superior wisdom, inspectors and advisers can get locked into a perpetual spiral of unproven innovation, but are not accountable for the results.

As far back as the early 1950's students in teacher training colleges were told that the 'Look and Say' method was the best and only way to teach reading. Phonics, which for years had been called "the tools of the trade", were discarded as being out of date. Most teachers, when taking up their first teaching post, had the advice and guidance of experienced teachers who helped them to realise the limitations of the 'Look and Say' method, a slow way of learning to decode written words when used alone. The need to combine it with phonic work was clear, as properly taught phonic rules speed up the decoding process. The misconceptions of these recently qualified teachers about phonic work soon vanished as they used it to help children to acquire a high standard of reading and spelling.

However this did not last and in the 1960's phonics no longer played an important part in reading development in many schools. Although 96 percent of our language is phonic the 'order of the day' was again only 'Look and Say'. The term 'teaching reading' became known as 'hearing reading'. Any word the child did not know in this latter situation was supplied by the teacher; then the child looked at the word, said it and tried to remember it. There was inadequate reinforcement of the learnt words, and no cross-checks to ensure that the child remembered the words. Other basic skills also suffered, as did simple tasks, such as learning the correct way to hold a pencil or pen, learning how to write and spell, knowing the names and sounds of the alphabet, and the writing of numbers properly. Much was neglected in favour of 'child-centred' activities advocated by many educationalists, themselves often the beneficiaries of a good, traditional primary education.

A recent survey carried out by the government-funded 'Adult Literacy and Basic Skills Unit', and published in 'Director' magazine, reported that one in four young adults aged between 16 and 20 has difficulty in reading and writing, and that 94 percent of them had received no help since they were 16 years of age. Projecting the results over the total young adult (16 to 20) population in England and Wales, the magazine estimated that about one million have problems with basic literacy and 1.5 million have problems with spelling. These figures caused no surprise to this author and indicated no significant change during a thirty year period.

The Reading Debate

Because there is no general agreement on the objectives of education, there can be no common ground on the adequacy or otherwise of current practice. One view of the education process in schools is that disciplined learning suppresses free expression, that competition is an anti-social force, and that standards should be dictated by the level of the weakest. An opposing view would reject those notions , and also claim that to prepare pupils for life after school there is a need to instil habits of study and hard work. Disagreement reigns on whether education is about process or outcomes, whether it should be child-centered or subject-centered.

There has not been and there is no national testing for reading skills, and current proposals for Standard Assessment Tasks in basic subjects at various ages in our schools are not intended for nor able to provide national statistical data on reading standards.

It is also difficult to compare reading performances between generations: one needs to ensure credible, representative samples, the tests have to be of identical difficulty, bearing in mind that word usage and frequency changes with time, and the tests must be carried out under the same, controlled conditions. Also, interpretation of results can be subjective: in a group of thirty people is it better to have all with a 50% score, or ten people with 70%, ten people with 50% and ten people with a 30% score?

Periodically, the media publish and comment on results of ad-hoc studies of reading skills, such as the one described above, which usually indicate falling standards. The blame for negative results is placed on one or more frequently-stated causes such as:- school strategies (classroom organisation, time allocated for reading and the teaching methods used), the introduction of unproven methods, teachers, teacher training, advisers, inspectors, and parents. This is followed by expert commentators discrediting the test procedures and the conclusions of the study, whilst others, equally expert, propose solutions based on their view of the source of the problem.

This media attention, which is focussed on these studies of the reading performance of our school children, is promoting the issue of a return in our schools to proper methods for, and emphasis on, the teaching of basic subjects – reading, writing, spelling and arithmetic. This issue is moving higher on the domestic political agenda.

Back to Basics

Hopefully, the current media and political attention to education, with the focus at Primary level on reintroducing the teaching of basic skills, will quickly lead to the implementation of sound policies in schools for the teaching of reading. Without discussing them in detail, the following four issues should be included in the debate:-

* inadequate time is devoted to the teaching of reading in Primary Schools
* teachers who are untrained in suitable teaching methods
* inadequate methods and/or improper use of suitable methods in many Primary Schools
* inefficient 'mixed ability' class policies

Over a thirty year period 'hearing reading' has prevailed instead of 'teaching reading', and a large number of pupils have left the school system without having acquired a proper foundation in reading. Every child passing through the normal state school system has all the abilities required to master the skill of reading; the system has failed any child who leaves school without learning to read properly.

Despite differing views on education, and the uncertain statistical basis for the current status of reading skills among various population groups, there can be no question of the desirability of acquiring the skill of reading. In particular, if Primary school children do not receive a sound foundation in reading, their performance in most other school subjects will inevitably suffer. If this situation is not corrected they will be at a disadvantage through the rest of their school days and beyond.

The number of tragic stories about the non-reader are legion. Until basic teaching of reading is restored, the tremendous exodus of children from our schools with few or no qualifications and a limited future will continue.

Appendix 5

Recommended Books

"Look, Say and Remember" Course

Two series of books are strongly recommended for the "Look, Say and Remember" course in Part 2 of the Teaching Programme. The first series entitled "One, Two, Three and Away", published by Collins Educational, covers the early stages of the programme. It has a good content level per page and good word repetition; this is very important at this level. The second series of books is entitled "The Beacon Readers". This series is superbly graded with good word repetition. Details of both series are given below.

First Series: "One, Two, Three and Away" by Sheila McCullagh

There are three sets of 'Main Books' comprising the series; each set can be ordered separately if required.

First Set of Main Books (Green Books)

No.	Catalogue No.	Title	Price (£)
1	0 00 313 169 6	The Village with Three Corners	0.95
1A	0 00 313 137 8	The Old Man and the Wind	0.95
1B	0 00 313 060 6	Gopal and the Little White Cat	0.95
2	0 00 313 107 6	Billy Blue-hat and the Duck Pond	0.95
2A	0 00 313 061 4	The Cat and the Feather	0.95
2B	0 00 313 062 2	Roger and the Ghost	0.95
		Second Set (Red Books)	
3	0 00 313 170 X	The Haystack	0.95
3A	0 00 313 063 0	The Donkey	0.95
3B	0 00 313 171 8	The Empty House	0.95
4	0 00 313 064 9	The Island in Deep River	0.95
4A	0 00 313 138 6	The Two Giants	0.95
4B	0 00 313 172 6	The House in the Corner of the Wood	0.95
		Third Set (Yellow Books)	
5	0 00 313 173 4	The Cat's Dance	1.65
6	0 00 313 065 7	The Stepping Stones	1.65
7	0 00 313 188 2	Billy Blue-hat's Day	1.65
8	0 00 313 189 0	The White Owls	1.65
9	0 00 313 066 5	The Lost Dog	1.65
10	0 00 313 074 6	The Three Robbers	1.65
11	0 00 313 190 4	A Boat on Deep River	1.65
12	0 00 313 174 2	The House in Dark Woods	1.65

Purchase

All the above books may be ordered from your bookseller, or by post from: Collins Educational, Freepost, Glasgow G4 0YX, Scotland; **Tel:** 041 772 3200

(The quoted prices are from the 1990 Catalogue).

Second Series: "The Beacon Readers" by James H. Fasset

The Beacon Readers recommended here have been used for many years with a very high success rate. There are several stories in each book. The stories, from many countries, are well-loved folk tales as well as fairy tales and legends, all of which children enjoy reading. The child who has completed the first series of books will find the first two books mentioned below very easy.

On completing these books, strongly helped by the Phonics Course, the child will have completed mechanical reading.

Purchase

Catalogue No.	Title	Price (£)
602 22506 X	Old Dog Tom	2.35
602 22507 8	Little Chick Chick	2.35
602 22508 6	The Pancake; Old Mother Hubbard (Two-book Set)	4.25
602 22509 4	Careful Hans; The Hobyahs; The King of the Birds (Three-book Set)	6.00
602 22510 8	Briar Rose; Rumplestiltskin; Dick Whittington (Three-book Set)	6.00
602 22511 6	William Tell; Androcles and the Lion; The Brave Little Tailor (Three-book Set)	6.90

All the Beacon Readers can be purchased separately and are published by Ginn & Co Ltd, Prebendal House, Parson's Fee, Aylesbury, Buckinghamshire HP20 2QZ. **Tel:** 0296 88411. They may be purchased from your bookseller, or by mail direct from the publisher; the above prices are from the 1991 catalogue **supplement.**

Optional books

"English Workbooks" by Ronald Ridout; published by Ginn & Co (address above). This is suitable for the age range 6–12 years.

This series of books represents a complete basic English Language course in ten graded workbooks. Each book is printed in colour and is clearly laid out leaving plenty of room for writing in the answers. It is also another aid to correct spelling. Prices are taken from the 1991 catalogue supplement; catalogue numbers are below:

Title	Catalogue No.	Price (£)
First Introductory	602 22385 7	0.75
Second Introductory	602 22386 5	0.75
Book 1	602 22387 3	0.95
Book 2	602 22388 1	0.95
Book 3	602 22389 X	0.95
Book 4	602 22390 3	0.95
Book 5	602 22391 1	0.95
Book 6	602 22392 X	1.00
Book 7	602 22393 8	1.00
Book 8	602 22394 6	1.00

"The Essential Spelling List" by Fred J. Schonell; published by Macmillan Education Ltd, Houndmills, Basingstoke, Hants RG1 2XS; **Tel:** 0256 29242. (This book is suitable for the age range 7–12 years). **Price** £1.50 plus post & packing.

"Basic Joined-up Handwriting" (A "Learn at Home" book) by Elizabeth Adams and Andrew Ross. Published by Longman Group UK Ltd, Longman House, Burnt Mill, Harlow, Essex CM20 2JE. **Prices:** Book 1: £1.99 Book 2: £1.99.

Bild links

Jalovec vom Sleme

Im Amphitheater des Sleme hat man – anders als im echten Theater – die beste Sicht auf den Jalovec von den obersten Rängen: vom Gipfel der Slemenova špica. Der Gras- und Latschengipfel ist zwar nur 1909 m hoch, kann es mit seinem Panorama jedoch leicht mit jenen der Julier-Größen aufnehmen. Schön zu überblicken sind der steile Anstieg durch den „Tamar" genannten Graben auf den Jalovec, seine Eisrinne und der rechts (nördlich) vom Jalovec befindliche Kot-Sattel, ein beliebtes Ziel für Skitourengeher.

Bild rechts:

Almrausch

Prächtige Almrauschbestände an der Slatnica, einer kleinen Scharte am Sleme. In den Julischen Alpen ist überwiegend die behaarte Alpenrose (Rhododendron hirsutum) anzutreffen. Sie wächst nur auf kalkhaltigen Böden. Ihr Erkennungsmerkmal sind die behaarten Blattränder, die wie Wimpern aussehen.

Jalovec

Bild links:

Auf dem Normalweg zum Jalovec. Unter der schattigen Šite Nordwand schlängelt sich der Weg im felsigen Kar aufwärts. Am Ende des immer schmäler werdenden Schuttfeldes wird die dunkle Wandflucht im Bereich der Jalovec-Scharte (Jalovška Škrbina) unterbrochen. Dort führt der gesicherte Normalweg aus der Rinne in die sonnige Ostseite der Goličica. Wer mit dem Jalovec ein stilles Abkommen treffen konnte, dass kein Steinschlag stattfindet, kann seinen Weg auch durch das sehr steile Couloir fortsetzen. Allerdings sollten sich nur bestens ausgerüstete und umsichtige Bergsteiger daran wagen.

Bild rechts:

Beim Ausstieg aus der schmalen Eisrinne trifft man wieder auf den Normalweg. Wie ein brüchiger Eckzahn ragt die 2394 m hohe Goličica aus dem Nebel heraus.

Bild links:

Loška Koritnica vom Jalovec Südgrat

Tiefblick vom Südgrat des Jalovec in das Tal Loška Koritnica mit der Ortschaft Log pod Mangartom. Durch den Wald im rechten Teil des Bildes schlängelt sich die Straße zur Grenze am Predil-Pass.

Jalovec von Log pod Mangartom im Herbst

Von Log pod Mangartom aus wird der atemberaubende Blick vom Gipfelgrat ins Tal verständlich: 1700 m fällt die Jalovec-Westflanke zur Koritnica ab. Der gerne als Abstieg genutzte Nordwestgrat ist links vom Gipfel zu sehen.

Am Gipfel des Jalovec

Im Rundblick vom Gipfel des Jalovec liegt links die wolkenfreie Mojstrovka. Am Horizont über den Wolken zeigen sich drei Gipfel: ganz links die Škrlatica; in der Mitte, nur wenig herausragend, der Razor und rechts die unverwechselbare Pyramide des Triglav.

Im Grün des Trenta-Tales unter den Wolken sitzt Julius Kugy aus Bronze und schaut herauf zum Gipfel des Jalovec.

Jalovec Nordwestgrat

Der schuttbeladene, steile Abstieg über den Nordwestgrat erfordert hohe Trittsicherheit. Rechts vom Grat des Jalovec der Bergkamm von der Veunza zur Hohen Ponca. Auf ihm verläuft die Grenze zwischen Italien und Slowenien.

Bild unten:

Frühlingsenzian

Unter den gleißend hellen Felsen des Jalovec bietet der Frühlingsenzian am Kot-Sattel den Augen eine erfrischende Abwechslung.

Bild rechts:

Gebirgsdynamik

Dass es in der für menschliche Dimensionen weitgehend ruhigen Gebirgslandschaft auch dynamisch zugehen kann, zeigt die Schleifspur dieses beachtlichen drei Meter hohen und fünf Meter breiten Felsbrockens im großen Schuttfeld unter dem Jalovec.

Blick ins Tal des Tamar und zur bewaldeten Sleme-Alm *(in Bildmitte rechts)*

Der Alpengarten „Juliana" in der Trenta

In der Trenta, nur 150 Meter nördlich der kleinen Kirche Santa Maria di Trenta findet man ein botanisches Juwel der Extraklasse. In einem rund 2600 Quadratmeter großen, heimeligen Steingarten gedeihen hier über 600 Pflanzen aus den Julischen Alpen. Dieses Alpinum wurde 1926 vom Triestiner Kaufmann Albert Bois de Chesne geschaffen, einem Bergfreund von Julius Kugy. Der Besuch der Anlage erfreut gewiss nicht nur botanische Spezialisten, denn die Vielfalt und Farbigkeit zahlloser Blumenarten der Julischen auf engem Raum ist für jeden Reisenden erholsam und lehrreich.

Pfingstrose

Frauenschuh

Akelei

Alpendistel

Zwerg-Alpenrose

Jalovec aus der Trenta

Wie nach Westen und Norden zeigt der kantige Jalovec auch nach Süden seinen ausgeprägten „Charakter“. Alle Anstiege fordern von dem, der ihn erobern will, Respekt, Kraft und Ausdauer.

Zadnja Trenta mit dem Bavški Grintavec

Von Wolken bedrängt grüßt der Bavški Grintavec ins hinterste Tal (Zadnja Trenta). Zu Zeiten als nur geschotterte Karrenwege in die Bergwelt vordrangen, war die Zadnja Trenta tatsächlich das „hinterste" Tal, weit weg von jeder größeren Siedlung. An der beruhigenden Einsamkeit hat sich nur wenig geändert. Die schützenden Wände der Berge vermitteln ein wohltuend heimeliges Gefühl fernab jeder lauten und technisierten Zivilisation. Von Ferne hört man das Rauschen der Soča, die aus einem Felstor über dem Tal das Licht der Welt erblickt.

Bilder oben:

Bavški Grintavec

Der Klettersteig durch die Nordwand des Bavški Grintavec erfordert wegen der Brüchigkeit des Gesteins höchste Aufmerksamkeit und Vorsicht. Dafür belohnt der Grintavec mit überraschenden Szenerien und einem fantastischen Gipfelpanorama.

Bild rechts:

Aus einer Nische des Klettersteigs sieht man vier der westlichen Julier am Horizont: ganz links den Kanin und in Bildmitte das Gipfeltrio Modeon del Buinz, Montasch und (heller) Wischberg.

Folgende Doppelseite: Panorama des Bavški Grintavec nach Osten

Škrlatica
Razor
Stenar
Bovški Gamsovec
Pihavec
Begunjski vrh
Rjavina
Triglav

Kanjavec
Prehodavci-Hütte
Malo Špičje
Veliko Špičje
Plaski Vogel

Soča

Alljährlich ist die Soča das Ziel der Wildwassersportler aus ganz Europa. Die Reinheit des Wassers macht das Fahren auf diesem Fluss zu einem edlen Erlebnis, die Frische der Fluten lässt jedoch gerne zu wärmendem Neopren greifen.

Südlich des Bavški Grintavec schneidet sich die Soča tief in den Kalkstein ein. Vor dem Talausgang der Lepena zeigt sie sich wieder offener und prunkt gleich mit der intensiven Farbe eines Aquamarins, der als Schmuckstück das Symbol der Reinheit darstellt.

An manchen engen Flusspassagen drängen seitlich zufließende Wasser ungestüm den Soča-Fluten zu, als könnten sie die Aufnahme in den Adelsstand reinsten Wassers nicht mehr erwarten.

Soča

Bild links:

Kann man sich eine schönere Badewanne vorstellen ? – Schöner kaum, in jedem Fall aber wärmer! Wesentlich wärmer!

Die Soča ist und bleibt eine Herausforderung für harte Kneipp-Jünger. Wenn schon Tropentage im Sommer zur menschlichen Grenzerfahrung in der Temperaturregulation einladen, sollten die wenigen Badeplätze mit ruhiger Strömung aufgesucht werden.

Bild rechte Seite:

Mit ihrem klaren Wasser und eingebettet in hellem Kalkstein und Sand wechselt die Soča ihre Farbe je nach Lichteinfall, Sonnenstand und Wassertiefe. Die Farbpalette reicht dabei von grün über aquamarinblau bis türkis.

Herbststimmung in der Trenta

Wer Farben liebt, besucht die Trenta im Herbst. Wie lodernde Flammen züngeln die gelben und roten Blätter der Bäume dem nahenden Schnee entgegen, der schon von der Nordwand des Plaski Vogel *(Bild rechts)* Besitz ergriffen hat. Kurz nur währt das Schauspiel, und der Winter ist lang.

Die Hängebrücken der Soča

Ein Hauch von Abenteuer schwebt über den Hängebrücken der Soča.
Sie sind die einzigen Verbindungswege zwischen der Straße und den verstreuten Höfen jenseits des Flusses. Inzwischen hat auch an der einsam in den Julischen Alpen gelegenen Soča moderne Bautechnik Einzug gehalten.
Solche malerischen Zeugen einer wackeligen und nicht ungefährlichen Vergangenheit machen immer mehr neuen und sicheren Übergängen Platz.
Zur Freude der Nostalgiker sind jedoch noch immer ein paar der romantischen Brücken übrig geblieben.

Herbststimmung in der Zadnja Trenta

Bild oben:

Der Winter schaut schon herab vom Prisank. Letzte Herbsttage laden zu einem Spaziergang ein, bevor sich das Winterweiß über die Landschaft legt und die stillste Zeit des Jahres beginnt.

Bild rechts:

Die Zadnja Trenta ist zu allen Jahreszeiten ein lohnendes Ziel. Ihr voller Charme kommt zur Geltung, wenn die Bäume farblich in Flammen stehen und der erste Schnee auf dem Bavški Grintavec den Kontrast noch steigert.

Slap Boka

Auf der Fahrtstrecke zwischen Bovec und Žaga wird an den südlichen Felswänden des Kanin der Boka-Wasserfall sichtbar. Was von den reichlichen Niederschlägen im porösen Karstgebiet des Kanin nicht versickert, stürzt im Slap Boka in einer über hundert Meter hohen Kaskade zu Tal und mündet in die Soča. Das akustisch und optisch eindrucksvolle Naturschauspiel kann auf zwei kurzen Steigen erreicht werden.

Bild links:

Razor aus der Trenta

Herbst im Flitscher Boden

Sein farbenprächtigstes Kostüm hat dieser Ahorn bei Flitsch (Bovec) angezogen. Wie groß war er im Jahr 1917, als sich genau an seinem Standort Österreicher und Italiener mit fürchterlichen Waffen bekämpften? Künden seine innersten Jahresringe vom Leid der Soldaten? Oder wagte er erst zu wachsen, als der ersehnte Friede ins Land zog? Den heutigen Generationen stellen sich neue Aufgaben: das Bewahren einer noch unverbrauchten Natur für eine friedliche und lebenswerte Zukunft in Europa. – Das wollte uns der Baum mitgeben und schüttelte ein paar seiner gelben Blätter auf unsere Schultern.

Die Gedenkkirche Javorca bei Tolmin

PAX – Friede – steht in großen Lettern auf der weißen Tafel mit der Sonnenuhr über dem Eingang zur Kirche Javorca.

Wahrlich, wenn man einen friedvollen Ort der Besinnung sucht, hier wird einem Ruhe zuteil: die Anlage der Kirche, ihre Lage, der Wärme ausstrahlende Holzbau und nicht zuletzt das Gedenken an die in den Bergen der Isonzofront im Ersten Weltkrieg gefallenen Soldaten wirken unglaublich beruhigend.

Die Heiliggeist-Gedenkkirche wurde 1916 noch während des Krieges von Soldaten der österreichisch-ungarischen Monarchie erbaut. Die gesamte Außenseite der Kirche ist mit meterhohen Tafeln versehen, auf denen die Wappen der zwanzig Kronländer des österreichisch-ungarischen Kaiserreiches abgebildet sind.

Die damit verbundenen Namen haben auf mich wie die erhebende Vorwegnahme eines vereinten Europa gewirkt. Wir hatten also schon einmal das, was im 3. Jahrtausend, freilich unter anderen Voraussetzungen und nach leidvollen Erfahrungen, endlich zusammenwächst. Die in großen Holztafeln an den Seitenwänden des Innenraumes eingebrannten 2564 Namen von Soldaten, die ihr Leben für „Kaiser und Vaterland" opfern mussten, berühren und stimmen sehr nachdenklich: Namen unterschiedlichster Klangfarben und sprachlicher Herkunft gemahnen sehr aktuell an eine damals wie heute schicksalhafte Gemeinsamkeit der Völker Europas. Der Innenraum ist jugendstilartig in Blau-, Schwarz-, Weiß- und Goldtönen verziert. Zwei große, kniende Engel an den Seitenwänden verstärken die friedvolle Atmosphäre.

Szabo János
Takács József
Török Sándor
Gefreiter:
Ágoston Péter
Csorba János
Csöke Péter
Erdei Károly
Füri József
Gaul Nikolaus
Bába István
Bakai János
Báló Antal
Bárkány József
Balta Mihály
Barna János

Kirche Javorca im Herbst

Ein strahlend schöner Herbsttag. Wir blicken nach Süden über das Tal der Tolminka.

Museum in Kobarid (Kobariški Muzej)

Eines der thematisch besten Museen Europas steht in Karfreit (Kobarid) im Isonzotal. Es ist in eindrucksvoller Weise den Ereignissen des Ersten Weltkrieges an der Isonzofront und in den Julischen Alpen gewidmet. Bereits die Eingangshalle *(Bild rechts oben)* mit Portraits von Soldaten aller beteiligten Armeen ist tief bewegend. Die Exponate, zahlreiche Originalaufnahmen und Modelle sind hervorragend präsentiert, was dem Museum neben anderen Auszeichnungen 1993 den Preis des Europarates einbrachte.

Krn

Die Westwand des Krn in der Nachmittagssonne, von Trnovo im Soča-Tal aus gesehen. Ein durch die Wand führender Klettersteig endet nahe der Hütte unter dem Gipfel. Typisch für den Krn ist seine dachartige Flanke, über welche der Anstieg von Süden in bequemen Serpentinen verläuft. Die nur 60 Meter unter dem 2244 m hohen Gipfel des Krn liegende Hütte (Gomišćkovo zavetišće na Krnu) ist während des ganzen 1000 m hohen Südanstieges zu sehen. Dem besonders bei Hitze nervenden Eindruck, dass die Hütte einfach nicht näher kommen will, begegnet der Wanderer am besten mit gesenktem Blick. Er wird dafür mit einer farbenprächtigen Blumenwelt entschädigt, die auch in den Julischen Alpen ihresgleichen sucht.

Bild links:

Dass es in manchen Jahren in den Julischen erhebliche Schneemengen gibt, zeigt ein Messpfahl in der Nähe der Krn-See-Hütte. Die bislang höchste Schneemenge wurde im April 2009 mit 3,50 Meter registriert.

Bild rechts:

Krn vom Krn-See

Ein langer Anstieg auf den Krn nimmt seinen Ausgang im Lepena-Tal. Auf 1400 m Höhe erreicht man ein Hochtal mit dem Krn-See *(Bild rechts)*. Auf dem Bergkamm am Horizont mit dem 2244 m hohen Krn verlief im Ersten Weltkrieg die Front.

Wenn schon im Oktober der erste Schnee fällt und der See zufriert, lässt sich erahnen, wie hart und lang die Kriegswinter für die Soldaten gewesen sein müssen.

Krainer Lilie mit Batognica

Sonnenröschen am Krn

Bild linke Seite:

Bergsteigende Blumen? – wie in einer Gruppenwanderung klettern Meisterwurz und Krainer Lilien die Südflanke des Krn empor.

Das Blumenwunder am Krn

Im Sommer zieht der Krn sein schönstes Blumenkleid an. Auf dem in vielen Kehren angelegten ehemaligen Militärweg zur Krnhütte kommen deshalb blumenverliebte Fotografen nur sehr langsam voran. Es gilt auch nicht, die über 1000 Höhenmeter zur Hütte rasch zu absolvieren, sondern sich dem stillen Genuss hinzugeben, die Vielfalt der Natur zu bewundern: Laserkraut *(Bild linke Seite)*, Schlangenknöterich *(Bild ganz oben)* und Steinnelke *(Bild oben)*.

Nächste Doppelseite:
In der Morgendämmerung auf dem Gipfel des Krn

Mangart
vorne: Bavški Grintavec
Jalovec
Mala Mojstrovka
Vršič-Pass
Prisank

Špik
Razor
Škrlatica
Stenar
Pihavec
Veliko špičje
Triglav
Tosc

Morgenstimmung am Gipfel des Krn

Bilder links:

Sonnenaufgang über dem südlichen Triglavgebiet

Bild rechts:

Morgendlicher Blick vom Gipfel des Krn nach Norden. Im Hintergrund mit den Schneeresten das Kanin-Massiv. Rechts davon schmückt sich der Montasch mit einer Wolkenhaube.

Rotes Seifenkraut in der Krn-Scharte

Abstieg vom Krn zur Batognica

Der Weg vom Gipfel des Krn zur 2165 m hohen Batognica verläuft über erfrischend grüne und blumenreiche Hänge, auf denen große Schafherden anzutreffen sind. Vor der kugeligen Batognica erkennt man in der Krn-Scharte (Krnska škrbina) noch die Reste ehemaliger Schützengräben aus dem Ersten Weltkrieg. Angesichts der friedvollen Stimmung an diesem Morgen mag man sich gar nicht vorstellen, wie es hier in den Jahren des sinnlosen Krieges ausgesehen hatte.

Krn von der Batognica

Der Südanstieg auf den Krn ist von der Batognica gut einsehbar. Am Grat links unterhalb des Gipfels ist die Krnhütte zu erkennen *(Bild rechts)*. Links unten die westlich von Kobarid gelegenen Wiesen und Felder.

Die Batognica ist mir vor allem deshalb in starker Erinnerung geblieben, weil bei unserem Besuch von ihr eine besonders intensive Ruhe auszugehen schien: so als wollte sie dem Wanderer genau das Gegenteil dessen vermitteln, was dieser Berg an menschlichem Leid und physischer Zerstörung im Ersten Weltkrieg erfahren musste (siehe *nächste Doppelseite*). Vielleicht war es aber auch nur die Sanftmut der Schafe, ihr ruhiges und zutrauliches Verhalten *(Bild links und oben)*, dass der Gipfel so besonders friedvoll wirkte.

Die Kavernen der Batognica

Welches Feindbild wurde den Soldaten der beteiligten Armeen im Ersten Weltkrieg mitgegeben, dass solche Stollensysteme unter widrigsten Bedingungen in das Innere der Berge vorangetrieben werden konnten? Der Minenkrieg auf der Batognica dauerte zwei Jahre lang an. Österreicher und Italiener durchlöcherten den Berg mit dem Ziel, mit Tonnen von Sprengstoff geladene Kavernen unter den gegnerischen Stellungen auszubauen. Die Anspannung unter den Soldaten muss enorm gewesen sein: Tag und Nacht lauschte jeder auf feindliche Bohrgeräusche aus dem Berginneren, denn die Kavernen dienten besonders im Winter den Soldaten auch als beschusssichere, doch modrige Unterkunft. Im September 1917 erschütterte eine gewaltige Explosion die Batognica, zerstörte die italienischen Gipfelstellungen und hinterließ ein riesiges Trümmerfeld mit mehrere Meter hohen Steinblöcken.

Mangart und Jalovec von der Batognica

Vor den das Bild beherrschenden Gipfeln des Mangart (links) und des Jalovec (rechts) erhebt sich der 2347 m hohe Bavški Grintavec mit ausgeprägten Gesteinsschichten.

Mangart vom unteren Weißenfelser-See

Sein schönstes Profil zeigt der Mangart nach Norden zu den beiden Weißenfelser Seen. Der Bergkamm vom Mangart über die Veunza bis zur Hohen Ponca umrahmt diese klaren grünen Seen in einem Halbrund. Dieses vermittelt einen heimeligen Eindruck, lädt ein, die Gegend zu erkunden, das Panorama auf sich wirken oder einfach die Seele baumeln zu lassen.

Mangart

Er lässt sein markantes Antlitz bis weit nach Kärnten leuchten.

In den vielen Jahren meines Bergsteigerlebens ist er mir wie kein zweiter Berg der Julischen Alpen ans Herz gewachsen. Nicht nur, weil ich so oft auf seinem Gipfel gestanden bin. Wohnt man in Villach, kann man sich seinen verlockenden Konturen, Wänden und Schneefeldern nicht entziehen. Er ist darüber hinaus für Villacher Bergsteiger der Wetterindikator der Julier.

Der italienische Weg *(Bild links)* bietet atemberaubende Tiefblicke in die tausend Meter hohe Nordwand. Der slowenische Weg *(rechts in Bildmitte)* verläuft in der deutlich sichtbaren Verschneidung und erreicht rechts vom Gipfel den Grat.

Der Mangart als Sportarena

Die Höhenstraße auf den Mangart zieht auch andere Alpinsportler an: Mountainbiker freuen sich auf eine 10 km lange Abfahrt; Gleitschirmflieger mit Ziel Log pod Mangartom (625 m) starten am Mali vrh beim vorletzten Parkplatz auf 1900 m Seehöhe.

Eisenhut

Silberwurz

Kugeldistel

Mangartflora

Die mautpflichtige Mangart-Höhenstraße führt durch mehrere Tunnels bis auf eine Seehöhe von 2050 m. Dem allzu eilig auffahrenden Wanderer, der nur die felsigen Kletterrouten vor sich sieht, entgeht jedoch auf den letzten Kilometern und buchstäblich neben der Straße eine vielfältige Blumenpracht, die Botaniker immer gerne hierher kommen lässt: Almrausch *(linke Seite, Bild links unten)* Glockenblume *(linke Seite, Bild rechts unten)* und vom Wind bewegte Gräser geben für den Beobachter noch ein farbiges Konzert vor dem Aufstieg zum Gipfel des Mangart.

Bild rechts:

Junges Mutterglück kann manchmal recht anstrengend sein. Unter dem Einstieg zum slowenischen Weg auf den Mangart trafen wir ein sichtlich erschöpftes Mutterschaf mit ihrem vor Kälte zitternden Lämmchen. Unsere Sorge, dass das Kleine die kalte Nacht nicht überleben würde, war unbegründet. Tags darauf trafen wir beide wohlbehalten wieder.

Mangart, slowenischer Weg

Eine wahre Himmelsleiter! Der slowenische Weg auf den Mangart (*Bild links*) bietet auf der ganzen Strecke eine fantastische Aussicht, wie im Bild rechts nach Nordwesten auf den Karnischen Hauptkamm und ins untere Gailtal in Kärnten.

Ich habe den Mangart immer spät nachmittags aufgesucht. Am Endpunkt der Mautstraße lockt schon der nahe Gipfel. Die verbleibenden 600 Höhenmeter werden so zu einer klassischen Kurztour. Dennoch ist der Hochgebirgscharakter dieses Berges sehr wohl zu beachten.

Westliche Julische Alpen vom Mangart

Im Bild blicken wir vom slowenischen Weg auf die Wischberg- und Montasch-Gruppe. Knapp neben dem gezackten Drachengrat des Montasch streckt dahinter der Bergkamm des Zuc dal Bôr seine kleine Nase in den Himmel. Er zählt bereits zu den Karnischen Alpen.

Nächste Doppelseite:
Föhnstimmung über dem Wischberg und dem Montasch

Östliche Julier vom Mangart

Auf der linken Seite des Bildes ragt der Triglav über den abendlichen Dunst hinaus. In der Bildmitte wendet der Jalovec dem Mangart seinen Nordwestgrat zu, eine gern genutzte Abstiegsroute zum Kotsattel.

Nächste Doppelseite:

Die Aussicht am Mangart ist in alle Himmelsrichtungen spektakulär. Links stehen Wischberg und Montasch friedlich beisammen.

Abendruhe

Der Mangart legt sich zur Ruhe. Langsam, gleichermaßen liebevoll, zieht ihm die Sonne die Decke der Nacht über sein Haupt. Ein leiser Wind streicht zärtlich über seine Wände und flüstert mit den Steinen. Wer die Berge liebt, hört daraus die Geschichten eines schönen Tages. Sie wecken in uns die schon als Kind empfundene Zufriedenheit, glückliche Stunden auf dieser Erde erlebt zu haben.

Über allen Gipfeln ist Ruh'

Die Abendstimmungen am Mangart sind von besonderem Reiz, ist doch der Abstieg so nach Westen geneigt, dass es sich bis zum Einbruch der Dunkelheit wandern lässt und die Stille nicht nur die Gipfel und Grate der Berge erfasst. Nach einem schönen Tag befällt auch eine glückliche Müdigkeit Herz und Seele.

West-Julier

Westlich vom Predilpass

Der flächenmäßig etwas kleinere Teil der Julischen Alpen ist der westliche, der an der Grenze zwischen Slowenien und Italien beginnt und sich westwärts bis zu den Flussläufen der Fella und des Tagliamento erstreckt. Am Raibler See ganz im Osten der Westjulier beginnen wir unsere Entdeckungsreise durch eine Bergwelt, die vielfach dreisprachige Namen aufweist. Der Grund dafür ist die Lage am Schnittpunkt der drei großen europäischen Sprachfamilien (Germanisch, Romanisch und Slawisch) und ihre im Lauf der Geschichte wechselnde staatliche Zugehörigkeit. In der deutschen Ausgabe dieses Bildbandes finden sich daher vorzugsweise deutsche Namen, sofern es solche gibt; ist ein deutscher Name nicht mehr bekannt oder wird er nicht mehr verwendet, wird der italienische/friulanische oder slowenische Name angeführt. Das Glossar auf Seite 262 führt zu den im Text erwähnten Gipfeln und Orten deren mehrsprachige Bezeichnungen an.

Stille am Raibler See

Links der Raibler Seekopf (ital. Cima del Lago / slow. Jerebica), der schneebedeckte Berg im Hintergrund ist die Cima Confine (slow. Črnelska špica).

Herbst am Raibler See

Unter dem Raibler Seekopf zaubert ein warmer Südwind die glitzernde Botschaft eines fernen Sommers in den Raibler See.

Winterstürme am Kanin

Wer möchte jetzt auf dem Monte Leupa/ Lopa im Kanin-Massiv stehen, wenn der Winter mit dem ersten Höhensturm seine monatelange Regentschaft anmeldet?

Die Gilberti-Hütte (Rifugio Gilberto) am Kanin

Tief unter den Nordwänden des Prestreljenik (Monte Forato) liegt die Gilberti-Hütte in der Nähe der Bergstation der Kanin-Seilbahn. Rechts oben im Bild ist im schattigen Grat das Felsenfenster des Prestreljenik zu erkennen. Die Gilberti-Hütte ist im Winter Ausgangspunkt schöner Skitouren im Kanin-Gebiet.

Sella Bila Pec von der Gilberti-Hütte

Bei lawinensicheren Schneeverhältnissen ist die Abfahrt von der Sella Bila Pec ein besonderer Genuss. Über diese Scharte verläuft der Sommerweg auf den Kanin und zum Monte Sart. Angesichts der im Bild tief verschneiten Hänge fällt es schwer, sich vorzustellen, dass im Frühling und Sommer hier ein wahres Blumenmeer die Besucher überrascht.

Nächste Doppelseite:

Almrausch am Weg zum Nordwand-Klettersteig auf den Kanin mit Blick zum Montasch (ital. Jôf di Montasio) und darunter liegender Pecol-Alm *(linke Bildseite)*. In der Mitte der rechten Seite überragt im Hintergrund der pyramidenförmige Gipfel des Wischberg (Jôf Fuart) die vor ihm liegenden Kastreinspitzen und die Felswand zwischen Cima de la Puartate und der Punta Plagnis.

Bilder linke Seite:

Kanin (Monte Canin)

Ausgangspunkt der Besteigung des Kanin über den Nordwand-Klettersteig (Via ferrata Divisione Julia – *drei Bilder links oben*) ist die Gilberti-Hütte nahe der Bergstation der Seilbahn vom Neveasattel. Der Weg zum Einstieg ist nicht nur im Bereich der Bila Pec ein botanischer Lehrpfad. Bis zum Kanin-Gletscher erfreuen unzählige Blumenpolster das Auge inmitten der sonst kargen Karstlandschaft. Besonders stark vertreten ist der Gelbe Alpenmohn. Der schöne Klettersteig endet in der Kanin-Scharte. Von ihr führt der julische Rundkurs nach Osten *(Bild rechts unten)* an einem vulkanähnlichen Schlund vorbei und südlich unter dem Bergkamm entlang zum Prestreljenik.

Bilder rechts und unten:

Das Prestreljenik-Fenster

Sogar von der Pecol-Alm ist das Felsentor im Grat des Prestreljenik auszumachen. Ob es wahr ist, dass der Teufel auf seinem Höllenritt über den Bergkamm ins jenseitige Soča-Tal etwas zu tief geflogen ist? Grün leuchten die Montasch-Almen herüber. Das Bild unten zeigt die Südansicht des Felsentors.

Kanin (Monte Canin) von der Pecol-Alm

Die Pecol-Alm ist die westlichste der Montasch-Almen, die sich unter den Südhängen des Montasch und Modeon del Buinz erstrecken. Der lange Grat von der Prevalascharte (am linken Bildrand) findet Richtung Westen seinen ersten Höhepunkt im 2498 m hohen Prestreljenik (ital. Monte Forato). In der Scharte rechts davon leuchtet der blaue Himmel durch das Prestreljenik-Fenster. Auf der rechten Seite des Bildes sind drei ausgeprägte Gipfel zu sehen: der Monte Ursic, der Kanin (Monte Canin), mit 2587 m als höchster in der Mitte und ganz rechts der 2441 m hohe Pico di Carnizza.

Im gesamten Karststock des Kanin befinden sich Eingänge zu Höhlensystemen, die zu den tiefsten der Welt zählen (bis zu 1400 m).

Rechts vom Kanin und dem Pico Carnizza verläuft der Weg zum Monte Sart.

Bild linke Seite, Bilder oben und unten:

Monte Sart

Der weite, doch großteils auf gleicher Höhe verlaufende Weg von der Sella Bila Pec oberhalb der Gilberti-Hütte zum Monte Sart *(Bild links)* sieht nur auf den ersten Blick öde und steinig aus. Der Monte Sart lockt mit einer vielfältigen Blumenlandschaft, die den langen Anstieg lohnt. Im Bild oben ein Enzian, das Bild unten zeigt die Gemswurz.

Bild rechts:

Storchenschnabelfeld auf der Forchia di Terrarossa vor dem Anstieg auf den Gipfel des Monte Sart.

Bild linke Seite:

Rombon

Blick von der Cima Confine über das Rombon Plateau. Ganz links der Jalovec, der dunkle Berg rechts ist der Rombon. Links neben ihm im Hintergrund der Triglav.

Bilder rechte Seite:

Kleine Confinspitze (Cima Confine piccola)

Italienische Stellungen aus dem Ersten Weltkrieg. Wie seltsam und unwirklich wirken doch diese von Menschen geschaffenen Bauten im Vergleich zu den Schöpfungen der Natur wie die Zois-Glockenblumen.

Panorama von der Prevala nach Norden

Von der Gilberti-Hütte (Rifugio Gilberti) auf der Prevala ist der lange Bergkamm vom Montasch über die Cregnedulflanke bis zur Weißenbachspitze im Blickfeld des Wanderers. Links unter dem Montasch erstrecken sich die weitläufigen Montasch-Almen. Der westliche Teil von ihnen, direkt unter dem Montasch, ist die Pecol-Alm, von der viele Touren ihren Ausgang nehmen.

Schnee-Enzian

Eisenhut

Blumen der Prevala

Die Julischen Alpen bieten den besonderen Reiz des kontrastreichen Nebeneinanders von felsiger Ödnis und üppiger Blumenpracht. Fotografisch an Blumen interessierte Wanderer sind besonders auf dem weiten Weg von der Prevala zum Rombon nahezu hilflos den ständig um die Gunst ihrer Aufmerksamkeit werbenden kleinen Naturwundern ausgesetzt.

Kanin (Monte Canin) von der Pecol am Morgen

Käserei auf der Pecol

Am nordwestlichen Ende der Pecol-Alm steht eine Käserei, die den köstlichen „Montasio"-Käse herstellt. Von dieser Almwirtschaft nimmt der Weg zum Monte Cimone seinen Ausgang.

Cima di Terrarossa von der Pecol

Die beliebte Tour auf die Cima di Terrarossa verläuft an der Brazza-Hütte (Rifugio G. di Brazza) auf dem kleinen bewaldeten Hügel vorbei und zieht dann in angenehmer Steigung in die breite, besonnte Wandflucht nach links. Es ist ein Höhenunterschied von 900 Meter zu überwinden, doch der Anblick der Steinböcke und die Aussicht sind es wert.

Wischberg und Kastreinspitzen von der Cima di Terrarossa

Hell strahlend grüßt der Wischberg zum Gipfel der Cima di Terrarossa herüber. Die Kastreinspitzen in der Bildmitte liegen im Wolkenschatten. Links unten im Tal befindet sich die Seisera.

Cima di Terrarossa

Im Revier an der Cima di Terrarossa fühlt sich der Wanderer ständig den argwöhnischen und doch zugleich gelassenen Blicken der Steinböcke ausgesetzt.

Bild links:

Abstieg zur Forca del Palone

Der Klettersteig (Sentiero) Augusto ed Elenita Leva von der Cima di Terrarossa zum Montasch bietet im senkrechten Abstieg zur Palone-Scharte (Forca del Palone) eine Eisenleiter.

Palone-Scharte (Forca del Palone)

Felsentore der Julier! Die Wege in den Julischen Alpen haben immer wieder überraschende Ausblicke zu bieten. Die senkrechten Felswände umrahmen den weiten Blick nach Norden, in das Tal der Seisera und zum Monte Lussari.

In der Südwestwand des Modeon del Montasio

Der Klettersteig Augusto ed Elenita Leva quert die südwestlichen Felsflanken des Modeon del Montasio und der Cima Verde. Er mündet in den Normalweg auf den Montasch.

Foronon del Buinz
Klettersteig Ceria Merlone

Nahe dem Gipfel der Cima di Terrarossa zweigt der Klettersteig Ceria Merlone nach Südosten zum Foronon del Buinz ab. An blumenreichen Wiesenhängen vorbei (*Bilder links:* Silberwurz und Alpengrasnelke) wird die Forca de lis Sieris erreicht *(Bild oben)*. Von dieser 2274 m hoch gelegenen Scharte im Bild rechts bietet sich eine überwältigende Aussicht auf den Großen Nabois (links), den Wischberg (Mitte) und die Kastreinspitzen. Jenseits der Moses-Scharte, die Wischberg und Kastreinspitzen trennt, lugt gerade noch der Gipfel des Mangart hervor.

Im Reich der Steinböcke

In Berg- und Wanderführern über die Julischen Alpen wird für einzelne anspruchsvolle Touren unbedingte Trittsicherheit vom Wanderer gefordert. Lässt dieser Begriff in der praktischen Umsetzung Interpretationen offen, dann ist eine Besteigung der Wände und Grate der Cima di Terrarossa, der Cime Gambon und des östlich davon gelegenen Foronon der Buinz angezeigt. Die Steinböcke geben dort eindrucksvolle Vorführungen. Sie sind die unübertroffenen Beherrscher der Vertikalen.

Bild links:

Auf dem Steig von der Cima di Terrarossa zu den Cime Gambon genießt man einen direkten Blick zum Kaninmassiv mit den Gipfeln des Monte Ursic, den 2587 m hohen Kanin (Monte Canin) und den Picco di Carnizza.

Foronon del Buinz

Bild links:

Rastplatz auf dem Ceria Merlone-Steig mit Blick zum 2402 m hohen Monte Leupa *(rechts im Bild)*. Im bewaldeten Tal liegt der Nevea-Pass.

Bild rechts:

Aufstieg zum Gipfel des 2531 m hohen Foronon del Buinz mit Blick zum Montasch. Trotz griffigem Fels und guter Drahtseilsicherung sollte für Klettersteiggeher die Selbstsicherung unverzichtbar sein. Rechts neben dem nordwestlich markant die Szenerie beherrschenden Montasch sind in der Ferne die schneebedeckten Hohen Tauern auszumachen. Die grüne Scharte links unter dem Montasch ist die Forca dei Disteis; die dunkelgrün bewaldeten Berge dahinter gehören zu den Karnischen Alpen.

Foronon del Buinz

Der Foronon del Buinz hat ein Herz für müde Wanderer: Der waagrechte Stein auf seinem Gipfel ist einer der schönsten – und bequemsten – Rastplätze der Julier *(Bild links)*. Hier lässt es sich geruhsam räkeln, und man hat zugleich die nahen Gipfel im Blick: den Wischberg, die begrünten Kastreinspitzen und den Modeon del Buinz, der südseitig auf einem Band umgangen wird. Am Horizont ragen vier Berge hervor: Der Mangart, die Škrlatica, der Jalovec und der Triglav. Ist nicht die Bährenlahnscharte und der Weiterweg zu den Kastreinspitzen das Ziel, kann man über den Monte Cregnedul und die blumenreiche Cregnedul-Alm *(Bild ganz oben)* zum Nevea-Pass absteigen. Auf dem Weg trifft man auch auf den Gefransten Enzian *(Bild oben)*.

Aufstieg zu den Kastreinspitzen

In der Bährenlahnscharte (Forc. Lavinal del Orso) findet der Merlone-Steig von der Cima di Terrarossa im Klettersteig Anita Goitan auf die Kastreinspitzen seine Fortsetzung. Von der Kaverne der ehemaligen Bergstation der Materialseilbahn auf die Kastreinspitzen öffnet sich ein direkter Blick zum 2666 m hohen Wischberg *(Bild ganz oben)*. Alle Anstiege auf die „Kastrein" führen durch farbenprächtige Blumenbestände, etwa dem Sonnenröschen *(Bild oben)*.

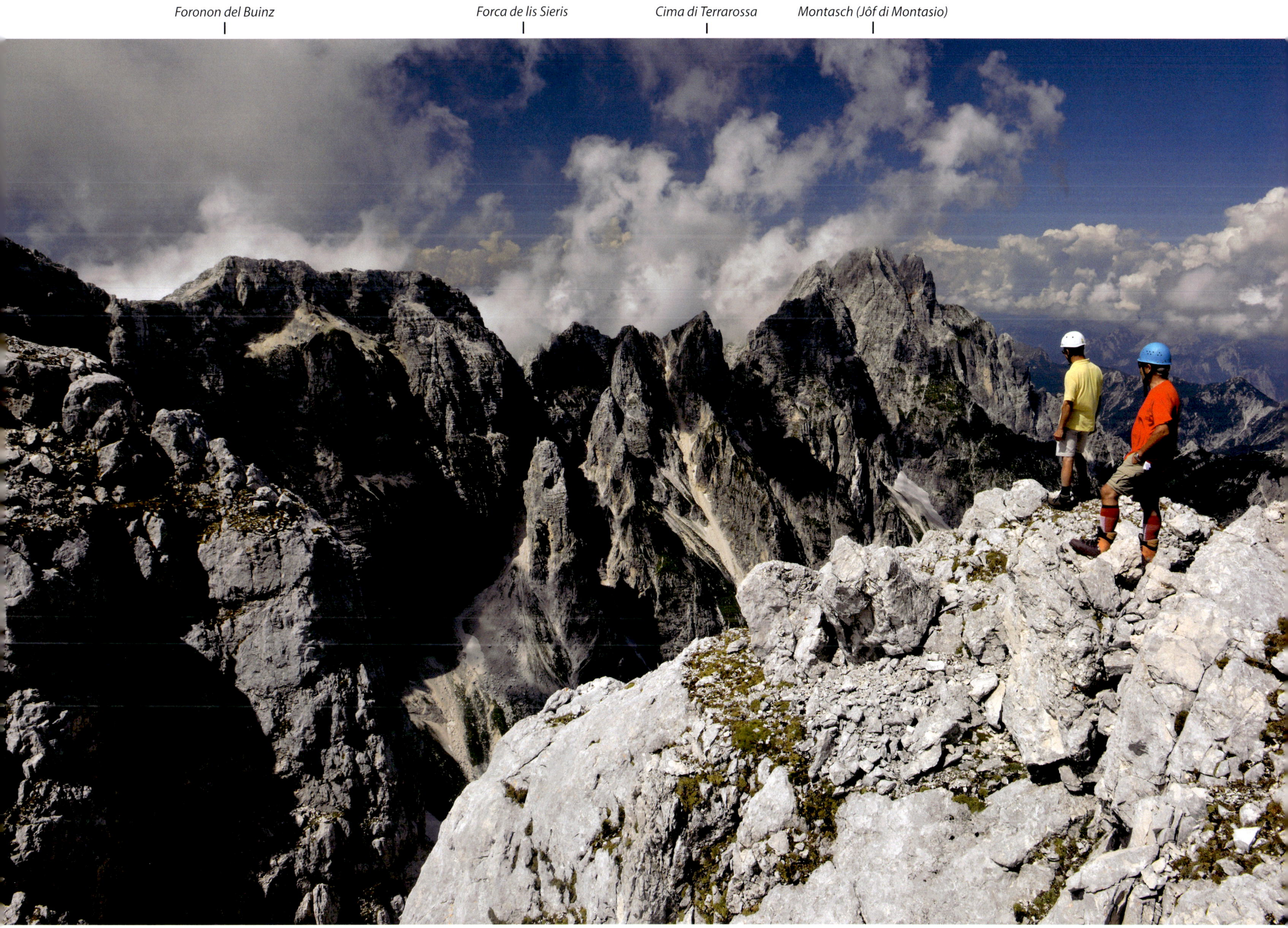

Westliches Panorama von den Kastreinspitzen (Cime Castrein)

Während die Österreicher die Kastreinspitzen von 1915 bis 1917 militärisch behaupteten, saßen auf den Graten gegenüber, vom Foronon del Buinz bis zum Montasch die Italiener. Über die Sinnlosigkeit eines Krieges im Allgemeinen und in einer schönen Bergwelt im Besonderen haben sich gewiss die Soldaten auf beiden Seiten immer wieder Gedanken gemacht.

Kastreinspitzen (Cime Castrein)

Der pyramidenförmige Wischberg *(Bild links)* und die Kastreinspitzen bildeten im Ersten Weltkrieg die Stützpunkte der Österreicher. Auch in diesem Teil wurden die strategisch wertvollen Gipfel und Grate ausgehöhlt, befestigt und mit Seilbahnen und Mannschaftsunterkünften bespickt. Welche waghalsigen Plätze dafür ausgesucht werden mussten, kann der Besucher der Kastreinspitzen heute noch sehen *(Bilder unten)*. Die Stützmauer ist noch zur Gänze erhalten geblieben, nur das Holz der Unterkünfte ist schon längst dem Gesetz der Schwerkraft über die darunter liegende senkrechte Wand gefolgt. Manche Überreste der nicht nur heute, sondern zu aller Zeit fragwürdigen Kriegsanstrengungen stechen wie ein mahnender Zeigefinger für kommende Generationen in den blauen Julier-Himmel *(Bild rechts)*.

Wie schön ist es doch, sich hier in den Julischen, die so viel Zerstörung ertragen mussten, mit Menschen anderer Sprache und Herkunft zu treffen. Uns eint etwas Hohes und Friedvolles:

Die Liebe zu den Bergen!

Wischberg (Jôf Fuart)

Der Klettersteig Sentiero Attrezzato Anita Goitan endet für die Kastreinspitzen mit dem Abstieg zur Moses-Scharte. Hier öffnet sich der Blick wieder zum Montasch *(Bild links)*. Links von der u-förmigen Scharte am Bildrand ist die spitze Cima di Terrarossa. Von der Moses-Scharte setzt sich der Anita Goitan-Steig auf den Wischberg fort *(Bild rechts)*.
Die beiden Gipfel im Vordergrund sind die Korspitze (Cima del Vallone) links und die Hohe Weißenbachspitze (Cima Alta di Riobianco) rechts.
Im dunstigen Hintergrund ragt der Jalovec über der schottrigen Korscharte auf. Ganz rechts und als höchster thront der Triglav. Vor ihm schiebt sich der langgestreckte Grat des Pelc ins Bild.

Wolkenspiel über dem Wischberg

„Das Schönste auf der Wanderschaft, das ist die süße Rast", schrieb Kugy in seinem Buch „Die Julischen Alpen im Bilde". Ergänzen möchte ich: „Das Schönste an der Rast, das ist ein Wolkenkino" *(Bild oben)*. Am Berghang zu lehnen, dem Spiel der Wolken zuzusehen und den kreativen Deutungen und Gedanken freien Lauf zu lassen! Im Zeitlupentempo laufen die spannendsten „Tierfilme" ab, die trotzdem herrliche Entspannung bieten. Die träg-flüchtigen Gebilde wandeln ständig ihre Form und gemahnen uns zur „Entschleunigung" unseres modernen Lebens, in dem Zeit mit Geld gleichgesetzt wird. Sehen wir nicht gerade einen bellenden Hund ?

Bild links:

Wischberg – Panorama nach Süden

Vom Klettersteig Anita Goitan sieht man den langen Bergkamm zwischen dem Rombon (links) und dem Monte Leupa (rechts). In Bildmitte links die Confinspitze (Cima Confine) und der Monte Cergnala.
Es ist nicht nur die Fernsicht, die das Auge des Wanderers fesselt. Im steilen Felsgelände auf den Weg zu achten, rückt die vielen Blumen auf den Grasinseln ins Blickfeld, wie das anderswo bereits selten gewordene Edelweiß.

Gamsnadel und Innominata im Gamsmuttergrat

Bild links:

Immer wieder überrascht der Anita Goitan-Klettersteig mit spektakulären Felsszenerien, wie der im Bild links am linken Bildrand sichtbaren Gamsnadel (ital. Ago dei Camosci). Rechts von der Scharte der von Kugy „Innominata" getaufte Kleinspitz. Der Anita Goitan-Klettersteig bietet hier eine Variante auf der Nordseite der Innominata. Der Zugang führt an dem im Bild links unter der Wolke am Grat erkennbaren Steinmann vorbei.

Bild rechts:

Auf der Südseite die Gamsmuttertürme querend endet der Sentiero Anita Goitan in der Kaltwasserscharte (Forca di Biofreddo). Der weitere Abstieg verläuft nach Süden zur Corsi-Hütte *(Rifugio Corsi).*

Steinerner Jäger (Cima del Cacciatore)

Bild links:

Die beste Aussicht in die riesigen Nordwände des Gamsmutterzuges und des Wischbergs genießt der Betrachter vom Gipfel des Steinernen Jäger (Cima del Cacciatore).

Nach der Schneeschmelze läuten die Soldanellen immer als erste den kommenden Frühling ein.

Wischberg und Montasch vom Steinernen Jäger
Der Rundblick zeigt rechts von der Glocke den Wischberg, ganz rechts die breite Nordwand des Montasch. In der Gratsenke zwischen beiden die kleine Cima di Terrarossa. Wem der Aufstieg über 1300 Höhenmeter aus dem Tal auf den 2071 m hohen Steinernen Jäger zu viel ist, kann es sich leichter machen: Mit der Gondelbahn auf den 1786 m hohen Monte Santo Lussari. Von dort sind es nur mehr 300 Höhenmeter – ein guter Rabatt an die Kondition angesichts dieses Panoramas!

Monte Santo di Lussari

Bild links:

Abendstimmung am Wallfahrtsort Lussari. Ganz links der Mangart und der Jalovec. Rechts vom Dorf der Steinerne Jäger (Cima del Cacciatore).

Bild rechts und unten:

Seinen besonderen Charme und Gemütlichkeit entfaltet der Lussari im Winter mit den meterhohen Schneewänden zwischen den Gasthäusern.

Jôf di Sompdogna

Bild links:

Der Montasch wendet seine gewaltige Nordwand zum Jôf di Sompdogna. Der Klettersteig „Via Amalia" verläuft durch die breite Rinne unterhalb des oberen Schneefeldes und endet beim Bivacco Suringar auf 2430 m in der Montasch-Westflanke.

Bild rechts:

Der weite Blick vom Jôf di Sompdogna nach Osten vermittelt gute Einblicke in die mächtigen Wandfluchten des Nabois, des Wischbergs und der Kastreinspitzen.

Mangart
Prisank
Razor
Jalovec
Triglav
Nabois Grande
Wischberg (Jôf Fuart)
Kastreinspitzen (Cime Castrein)
Bährenlahnscharte
Forc. Lavinal dell'Orso

Montasch (Jôf di Montasio) von der Pecol-Alm

Im Bergkamm leuchtet der Montasch ganz links schon in der Morgensonne, während die Cima di Terrarossa, ganz rechts im Bild, noch im Schatten liegt. Der Normalweg auf den Montasch nimmt seinen Ausgang von der Pecol-Alm und verläuft über die begrünte Scharte links des Gipfels (Forca dei Disteis). In den Schuttfeldern unter der Südwand und im Bereich der Forca dei Disteis hat sich der „Herrenclub" der Steinböcke etabliert. Die „Damenrunde" mit den Jungen ist vorwiegend im Bereich des südlichen Anstiegs auf die Cima di Terrarossa anzutreffen.

An der Forca dei Disteis zweigt der Findenegg-Weg ab, der von der Südseite des Montasch in die Westflanke wechselt und beim 2430 m hoch exponiert unter den Wänden gelegenen Bivacco Suringar auf den Nordwand-Klettersteig „Via Amalia" trifft.

Am Findeneggweg des Montasch

Bild links:

Manche Steinböcke mögen gedrungen aussehen und doch blamieren sie mit ihrer Gewandtheit im steilsten Fels uns Menschen mitsamt unserer hoch entwickelten Bergausrüstung.

Das Bild links, vom Standort des Bivacco Suringar aufgenommen, bietet neben einem Tiefblick in das Dognatal auch eine weite Sicht bis zu den schneebedeckten Hohen Tauern am Horizont.

Bild rechts:

Nach der steilen Rinne in der Montasch-Westflanke trifft der Findeneggweg auf den Gipfelgrat.

Der grüne Berg ohne Wolkenhaube ist der Monte Schenone.

Nächste Doppelseite:

Der Gipfel des Montasch. Rechts ist das lang gestreckte Massiv des Kanin zu sehen.

Am Gipfel des Montasch (Jôf di Montasio)

Das Bild oben zeigt den Blick nach Osten. Der Wischberg wird vom Sockel der Glocke verdeckt. Die Wolken legen sich wie eine Meeresbrandung an den Foronon und Modeon del Buinz. Davor, als kleinster „Zahn" im langen Bergkamm herüber zum Montasch hebt sich die sonnige Flanke der Cima di Terrarossa gegen den Schatten ab.

Bild rechts:

Weit reicht der Blick nach Westen, hat doch der Montasch, mit 2753 m zweithöchster Berg der Julischen Alpen, zur Abendsonne hin nur mehr Gipfel um sich geschart, die 400 m niedriger sind. Nur der Monte Cimone ragt an diesem schönen Tag mit seinen 2379 m noch aus dem Wolkenmeer heraus. Der lang gestreckte, dunkle Höhenzug in der linken Bildhälfte ist der Monte Sart mit 2324 m.

Montasch (Jôf di Montasio)

Der Abstieg vom Gipfel des Montasch hat teilweise den Charakter eines Panoramaweges. Besonders stimmungsvoll ist die Wanderung am Abend, wenn die Sonne tief steht und die Konturen an Schärfe gewinnen. Blick nach Süden zum Kanin *(Bild links).*

Bild rechts:

Der Wischberg (Jôf Fuart) wird links von der Nabois-Scharte (Sella Nabois) und rechts von der Moses-Scharte (Forcella Mose) begrenzt.

Nächste Doppelseite:

Einen die Seele beruhigenden Anblick bietet das abendliche Wolkenspiel an der Forca dei Disteis, südlich des Montasch.

Eine kleine Madonna am Montasch

Beim Abstieg auf dem Normalweg durch die Südflanke des Montasch stießen wir auf eine markante Felsformation *(Bild rechte Seite)*. Wie überrascht waren wir jedoch, als wir uns dem Felsen näherten: eine kleine Madonnenfigur ganz in der Farbe des sie umgebenden Gesteins und deshalb völlig unscheinbar, fesselte unerwartet unseren Blick *(Bild oben)*. Was mag wohl der Bergsteiger empfunden haben, dem es ein Anliegen war, gerade hier dieses Zeichen zu setzen? Den ohnehin schon sehr malerischen Rastplatz umgab mit einem Male eine spirituelle Atmosphäre, die uns tief bewegte. Der Ort beeindruckte uns so sehr, dass wir hier verweilten, bis die Sonne unseren Augen entschwunden war. Schweigend und nachdenklich setzten wir in der einbrechenden Dämmerung unseren Abstieg fort.
In den westlichen Juliern sind an einigen Plätzen kleine Madonnenfiguren in unterschiedlichen Farben anzutreffen. Keine jedoch hatte uns so berührt wie diese am Montasch.

Abend am Montasch

Die Schatten der Nacht tasten sich mit langen Fingern durch die Schluchten des Montasch empor *(Bild links)*. Bald büßen auch die Zinnen, Grate und Wände ihre warme Farbe ein und hüllen sich in graues Dämmerlicht. Hinter dem Monte Cimone *(oben in Bildmitte)* fließt der Nebel wie in einem Wildbach zu Tal. Das sind die besinnlichen Stunden in den Julischen: Wenn man die Bergeinsamkeit genießt und dadurch Kraft für den nächsten Tag findet.

Italienische Stellungen im Dognatal

Das Dognatal war im Ersten Weltkrieg von höchster strategischer Bedeutung. Über die 15 km lange Straße (*Bild oben:* der Ort Chiout Zucuin vom Cuel de la Bareta) wurde der Nachschub zu den italienischen Truppen auf dem Sompdognasattel transportiert. Gleichzeitig befürchtete die italienische Militärführung einen Durchbruch der Österreicher durch das Dognatal. Dementsprechend stark bauten die Italiener daher die Verteidigungsstellungen zur Sicherung der Straße aus *(Bilder links)*. Die in die Berghänge getriebenen langen Tunnel dienten dem Schutz der Soldaten vor direkter Feindeinwirkung. Im Umfeld der Schützengräben hat sich die Natur das Gelände großteils wieder zurückerobert, was die Frage nach dem seinerzeitigen „Wozu?" noch dringlicher stellt.

In den Kavernen von Plans im Dognatal

Die Stollen der Verteidigungsanlage beeindrucken durch ihre Weitläufigkeit. Heutzutage diese Anlage zu besuchen, erscheint wegen der sehr brüchigen Stollenwände und der Gänge voller Abbruchmaterial nicht mehr ratsam.

Cuel de la Bareta

Im Canal del Ferro (Eisental) liegt der Ort Dogna am Eingang des nach ihm benannten Tales. Der erste Gipfel der Bergkette südlich des Dognatales ist der 1522 m hohe bewaldete Cuel de la Bareta. Er beherrscht durch seine strategisch günstige Lage das gesamte Tal bis zum Sompdognasattel, über welchen die Front verlief. Der während des Ersten Weltkrieges errichtete Artilleriestützpunkt zählte zu den wichtigsten militärischen Bauten der Italiener in den Julischen Alpen. Die Bedeutung dieser Stellung wurde dadurch betont, dass sogar der italienische König Vittorio Emanuele III. einmal die dort stationierten Truppen besuchte. Regelrecht ausgehöhlt wurde der Berg, um für neun Geschützkavernen, drei Munitionsdepots sowie für Verbindungsgänge und Unterkünfte Platz zu schaffen *(Bild links unten und auf der rechten Seite)*. Der Munitionstransport erfolgte mittels einer Seilbahn von Cadramazzo im Canal del Ferro aus. Die gewaltigen Reste der Bergstation sind heute noch erhalten *(Bild links und unten)*.

Montasch vom Monte Schenone

An einem warmen Herbsttag im Oktober. Vom Aufstieg zum Monte Schenone überblickt man den gesamten Höhenzug vom Montasch zum Monte Cimone (rechts im Bild). Links des dürren Baumes macht sich noch der Gipfel des Wischbergs bemerkbar. Der Monte Cimone wirft bereits seine Schatten in das Dognatal. – Wie schön ist es doch noch hier in der Sonne!

Monte Cimone

Forca Vandul, das „Höllentor"

Nach dem Aufstieg von der Pecol-Alm über den Weg 640 zur Scharte Forca Vandul steht der Wanderer so unvermittelt vor der atemberaubend ins Dognatal abfallenden Schlucht, dass die Bezeichnung „Höllentor" verständlich wird.

Monte Cimone von der Forca de la Viene

Von der Forca Vandul leitet ein Klettersteig auf den Grasrücken der Forca de la Viene. Über die neue Biwakschachtel „del Torso" schweift der Blick zu den Hohen Tauern im Nordwesten. Es ist Herbst. Das Gras hat sein Grün den ersten Nachtfrösten geopfert.

Monte Cimone

Bild links:

Vom Grasrücken der Forca de la Viene auf 2124 m hat man einen guten Einblick in die gewaltigen Nordwände beiderseits der Forca di Vandul.

Bild links:

Gipfelpanorama des Monte Cimone nach Osten. Der Montasch erglüht im letzten Abendlicht, rechts über den Talnebeln empfängt auch der Kanin noch ein wenig Sonne.

Bild rechts:

Auch der 2379 m Monte Cimone hat im Westen keinen Bergnachbarn mehr, der ihm die Abendsonne verstellen könnte. Die früher auf seinem Gipfel stehende Biwakschachtel „Bivacco Sandro del Torso" wurde aufgelassen und auf die 200 m niedrigere Forca de la Viene verlegt. Sie hat jedoch ihren Ruf als Panorama-Biwak erhalten *(Seite 250)*.

Abendpanorama vom Monte Cimone

Bis zu den Dolomiten reicht die Sicht an diesem schönen Abend! Die höchste Spitze der dunklen Bergkette im Vordergrund ist der 2195 m hohe Zuc dal Bôr. Er gehört zu den Karnischen Alpen.

Die Kirche Santa Anna di Carnizza

Das kleine Kirchlein auf der Sella Carnizza und *(Bild rechte Seite)* vom Monte Nische aus.

Abschied am Matajur

Auf unserer Wanderung durch die Julischen Alpen sind wir am südwestlichen Ende dieser großartigen Berglandschaft angekommen.

Der Matajur liegt nicht nur 45 Kilometer von der Adria bei Monfalcone entfernt, er bietet als letzter und nur 1645 m hoher Berg vor der Friulanischen Ebene eine unvergleichliche Fernsicht. Genau die richtige Kurztour zum Ausklang eines erlebnisreichen Bergjahres.

Vom Matajur schauen wir auf die julischen Vorberge, die letzte Gipfelkette vor der Tiefebene bei Udine *(nächste Doppelseite)*.
Sie hat uns auf unseren Touren wahrlich verwöhnt und den Juliern, den Bergen am Südrand der Alpen, ihr eigenes Licht verliehen: die Adriasonne. Am Matajur lassen wir es gut sein und schauen ihr noch beim Schlafengehen zu. In glutroter Dämmerung schickt sie uns ihren letzten Gruß auf unserem Abstieg. Die „Zivilisation" ruft uns mit ihren Lichtern *(übernächste Doppelseite)* zur Heimkehr.
In unseren Gedanken schweifen wir noch einmal zurück an den Ausgangspunkt unseres Streifzuges durch diese Bergwelt:
Zu den Narzissenwiesen der Golica, den Sternennächten am Triglav und den „küssenden Steinen" der Prehodavci; zum Vratatal mit dem zu Eis erstarrten Peričnik-Wasserfall, zur Škrlatica mit den Biwak-Mäusen und zum stillen Wocheinersee im Herbst; Erinnerungen werden wach an die vielen Blumen im Sieben-Seen-Tal, auf dem Krn und auf der Kastreinspitze; Das schwarzbraune, zutrauliche Schaf der Batognica hat sich ebenso ins Herz geschlichen wie die im steilen Fels herumtollenden jungen Steinböcke auf der Cima di Terrarossa und die Dohlen auf den Gipfeln mit ihren aerodynamischen Kunststücken.

Allesamt beglückende Augenblicke, in unserer Erinnerung gespeichert und bereichernde Erfahrungen, die für ein Leben lang reichen.

Diese herrlichen Berge heißen alle jene willkommen, die mit wachen Augen offen sind für Neues und die etwas heute Seltenes hören wollen:
die Stille!

Zu ihr wollen und werden wir zurückkehren:

In die Julischen Alpen.

Abstieg vom Matajur

Welch ein schöner Ausklang eines Bergjahres!
Am Kanin liegt schon Schnee und der südlichste Bergkamm der julischen Voralpen mit dem leicht angezuckerten Stol schiebt seine Abhänge unter die Nebeldecke der friulanischen Tiefebene. Die Federwolken hat ein kosmischer Künstler an den blauen Himmel komponiert. Wollen wir wirklich schon ins Tal?

Heimkehr

Die pulsierenden Lichter der Städte um Udine lassen uns an zu Hause denken. Doch für Bergsteiger in den Julischen Alpen gilt: vor der Heimkehr noch eine Einkehr! – In ein gutes Restaurant.

Orts- und Bergnamen in drei Sprachen

deutsch	slowenisch	italienisch	deutsch	slowenisch	italienisch
Bährenlahnscharte		Forcella Lavinal del Orso	Mangart	Mangrt	Mangart
Confinspitze	Črnelska špica	Cima Confine	Montasch	Špik nad Policami	Jôf di Montasio
Flitsch	Bovec	Plezzo	Monte Cimone	Strma peč	Monte Cimone
Flitscher Grintouc	Bavški Grintavec		Moses-Scharte		Sella (Forcella) Mose
Gamsmutter		Madre dei Camosci	Nevea-Pass	Nevejski prevo	Sella Nevea
Gamsnadel		Ago dei Camosci	Prisank	Prisojnik	
Hohe Ponza	Visoka ponca	Ponca Grande	Raibl	Rabelj	Cave del Predil
Isonzo	Soča	Isonzo	Raibler See	Rabelsko jezero	Lago del Predil
Jalouc	Jalovec	Jalouc	Seekopf (Raibler)	Jerebica	Cima del lago
Kahlkogel	Golica		Steinerner Jäger	Kamniti lovec	Cima del Cacciatore
Kanin	Visoki Kanin	Monte Canin	Tolmein	Tolmin	Tolmin
Karfreit	Kobarid	Caporetto	Veldes	Bled	
Kastreinspitze	Koštrunove špice	Cime Castrein	Veunza	Vevniza	Veunza
Kleinspitz		Innominata	Weißenbachspitze		Cima Alta di Riobianco
Köpfach	Krniška glavica	Jôf di Sompdogna	Weißenfelser See(n)	Mangartski jezeri	Lagi di Fusine
Krn	Krn	Monte Nero	Wischberg	Viž	Jôf Fuart
Kronau	Kranjska gora		Wochein	Bohinj	
Luschari	Sveti Višarje	Monte Santo di Lussari	Wocheiner See	Bohinjsko jezero	

Landkarten

Für die topographische Zuordnung der im Buch verwendeten Ortsangaben und Tourenbeschreibungen sind folgende Landkarten hilfreich:

Julische Alpen im Überblick

Julijske Alpe, Verlag SIDARTA, 1 : 50.000, © Geodetski inštitut Slovenije 2009, Ljubljana.

Triglavski Narodni Park, Planinska Zveza Slovenije, 1 : 50.000, © Kartografski oddelek 2006, Ljubljana

Östliche Julische Alpen

Nationalpark Triglav, © Freytag - Berndt u. Artaria, Wanderkarte 5141 , 1 : 35.000, Wien.

Für das Triglav-Gebiet, das Sieben-Seen-Tal, Prehodavci, Wocheinersee, Bavški Grintavec, obere Soča:

Bohinj, Verlag SIDARTA, 1: 25.000, © Geodetski Inštitut Slovenije 2010, Ljubljana.

Für das Triglav-Gebiet, Sieben-Seen-Tal, Prehodavci, Malo Špičje, Wocheinersee, Wocheiner Almen, Bovški Gamsovec, Razor, Škrlatica, Prisank:

Triglav, Planinska zveza Slovenije, 1 : 25.000, © Geodetski Inštitut Slovenije, Ljubljana.

Gebiet östlich des Triglav bis Bled, Wocheiner Almen:

Bled, tourist map, 1 : 30.000, Geodetski Inštitut Slovenije.

Für das Gebiet Kobarid, Krn, Batognica, Kirche Javorska, Tolmin, mittlere Soča:

Krn, Wanderkarte (Planinska karta) 1 : 25.000, © Geodetska uprava Republike Slovenije 2009

Für Jalovec, Mangart, Mojstrovka, Sleme, Prisank, Bavški Grintavec, Obere Soča, Trenta:

Mangart in Jalovec, 1: 25.000, © Geodetski inštitut Slovenije, Ljubljana

Westliche Julische Alpen

Topographische Wanderkarte
TABACCO 1: 25.000

Foglio/Blatt 18: Pontebba, Dogna-Tal, Cuel de la Bareta, Monte Schennone, Monte Cimone, Montasch.

Foglio/Blatt 19: Montasch (Jôf di Montasio), Cima de la Terrarossa, Pecol-Alm, Foronon del Buinz, Kastreinspitzen, Wischberg, Kanin, Mangart.

Alpe Giulie: Alle Gipfel von Blatt 18 und 19

Foglio/Blatt 27: Julische Voralpen, Monte Nische, Sella Carnizza, Cuel della Bareta, Monte Cimone, Montasch, Foronon del Buinz, Kastreinspitzen, Wischberg (Jôf Fuart), Kanin

Foglio/Blatt 41: Matajur, mittlere Soča, Krn

Danksagung

Besonderen Dank schulde ich meinem treuen Bergkameraden Günther Lang. Der exzellente Mozart-Kenner hat mir auf unseren Touren nicht nur viel Wissenswertes aus der klassischen Musik vermittelt; er stand mir bei der schwierigen Auswahl der Bilder ebenso zur Seite wie auch in der Layout-Phase als äußerst konstruktiver Kritiker und Erstlektor. Sein außergewöhnliches Einfühlungsvermögen hatte viele Aufnahmen erst möglich gemacht, denn bergsteigende Fotografen sind bei ernsthafter und deshalb zeitraubender Ausübung ihrer Tätigkeit sehr auf das Verständnis der Bergfreunde angewiesen. Da ist es schon ein Glück, wenn der Freund ebenfalls zur Stirnlampenfraktion unter den Bergsteigern zählt, die ihre Nachtruhe für erlebnisreiche Touren und besondere Bildmotive flexibel gestalten können.

Dem Verfasser informativer Wanderführer über die Julischen Alpen und über Friaul – Julisch Venetien, Helmut Lang, danke ich für die im Jahr 2009 an mich gestellte Frage, warum ich nicht eine moderne und farbige Ausgabe von Julius Kugys Standardwerk „ Die Julischen Alpen im Bilde" machen wolle. Damit gab er mir den auslösenden Impuls zu genau dem Buchprojekt, welches ich schon über 20 Jahre lang ohnehin im Kopf hatte.
Bei Dietlinde Lang bedanke ich mich, mir bei den Blumennamen Sicherheit gegeben zu haben.

Unter meinen langjährigen Bergkameraden, meinem Bruder Gerhard, Herbert Arbesser, Wolf Lang, Sepp Kircher und Raimundo Maia Júnior fand ich mit Dankbarkeit das Verständnis und die Geduld für meine fotografisch bedingten Entschleunigungen unserer Touren.

Christine Ratschnig war mir äußerst hilfreich, mich im Dschungel von Grafik-Programmen für das Layout zurechtzufinden.

Dem Verlagsleiter von Leykam, Dr. Wolfgang Hölzl, danke ich für die spontane Begeisterung und Annahme des Buchprojekts.

Bei Igor Stanonik und Janez Maselj von Gorenjski Tisk bedanke ich mich für die Unterstützung und Beratung in der Zeit der Druckvorbereitung.

Meiner Familie, meiner Frau Reini und meinen Töchtern Karin und Christine, bin ich dankbar, dass ich viel für die Familie bestimmte Freizeit der Arbeit am Buch widmen durfte und dass ich in der Schlussphase des Projekts nur die „Gelbe" und nicht die „Rote" Karte zu sehen bekam.

Hinweis: Die im Bildband gezeigten Touren sind fotografische Erlebnisberichte aus den Julischen Alpen. Die beschriebenen Touren nachzugehen, geschieht auf eigenes Risiko und enthebt den Leser nicht der Verantwortung für die eigene Sicherheit durch umsichtige Planung, Beachtung der Witterungsverhältnisse sowie eine tour-adäquate Einschätzung des Leistungsvermögens. Autor und Verlag übernehmen keine Haftung für etwaige Schäden und Unfälle.

An die Leserinnen und Leser: Aufgrund der besseren Lesbarkeit wurde auf die gleichzeitige Verwendung der weiblichen und männlichen Form im Text verzichtet.
Mit „ Wanderer" oder „Besucher" etc. sind natürlich immer beide Geschlechter angesprochen.

Impressum

Fotografie, Text und Layout: Helmut Teissl
Lektorat: Mag. Josef Schiffer
Druck und Endfertigung: Gorenjski tisk, Kranj, Slowenien
Gesamtherstellung: Leykam Buchverlag Graz

ISBN 978-3-7011-7759-2

1. Auflage

Titelbild: Blick vom Veliki Draški Vrh zum Triglav
Bild Umschlagseite 4 (hinten): Das Kugy-Denkmal in der Trenta, Blick zum Jalovec.
Musterbilder Umschlagseite 4 (hinten):
Zajamniki-Alm im Winter
Mangart am Abend
Herbst am Wocheinersee
Gelber Alpenmohn unter dem Kanin
Vorsatz: Hohe Ponca, Jalovec und Mangart im Morgenlicht vom Dobratsch
Bild Seite 263: Jalovec vom Sleme
Bild links, Seite 264: Mondnacht am Mangart
Nachsatz: Abendstimmung von der Südseite des Montasch. Blick zur Forca dei Disteis, zur Curtissons, Monte Zabus und Monte Cimone

Leykam Buchverlagsges.m.b.H. Nfg. & Co. KG
http://www.leykamverlag.at